THE NEW FEMALE ACTION HERO

JOE GOODWILL

The NEW FEMALE Action HERO

AN ANALYSIS OF FEMALE MASCULINITY IN THE NEW FEMALE ACTION HERO IN RECENT FILMS AND TELEVISION SHOWS

JOE GOODWILL

For Maggie, my wife and muse, and Sidney, my mother

CONTENTS

CHAPTER 1

A BRAVE NEW WORLD
OF BRAVE NEW WOMEN

SIGOURNEY WEAVER THRILLED MOVIE-GOERS WORLDWIDE as Warrant Officer Ellen Ripley, heroically confronting the most fearsome creatures that had ever scarred the silver screen in *Alien*, released in 1979. She and her audiences enjoyed it all so much that she came back and battled the creatures again in 1986 – and in 1992, and in 1997. Ripley was the first big screen female action hero,[1] and became an enduring role model for an entire generation of girls. For example, one young female reviewer notes: "Ellen Ripley is the best role model a girl could wish for" (Horrorist 2003). Similarly, another internet reviewer writes: "In *Alien* ... Ripley definitely takes a deserved place in the Heroine Content Hall of Fame beside *The Long Kiss Goodnight*'s Samantha and ... *Terminator 2*'s Sarah Connor" (Grace 2007). Another critic summed it up: Ripley is "an exemplary figure for women in her rugged independence, cool courage under fire, and resourcefulness" (Bundtzen 1987: 12). A review in *Glamour* – a popular magazine not known for its feminist stance –

1

enthused about the first three *Alien* films, noting that they "are just sci-fi popcorn movies, but their effect on female moviegoers has been profound. Ripley, in her no-nonsense cotton tank-top bodysuit, is the first woman we've seen left standing when all the guys are dead" (Krupp 1992: 163).

While Ripley was the first female hero of the celluloid screen, other equally impressive women soon joined her. In 1991 millions of movie-goers cheered as a buff, steely-jawed Sarah Connor, played by Linda Hamilton, fearlessly kicked robotic butt in *Terminator 2: Judgment Day*. Both Ripley and Sarah Connor embody what I call "female masculinity".[2] They also embody a new archetype that I refer to as the new female hero. Both of these concepts will be developed and explained in this chapter.

Ripley and Sarah Connor display the traditionally masculine characteristics of strength and courage, while carrying out heroic missions: Ripley protects the earth from alien invasion, and Sarah Connor leads a mission to save the world[3] from nuclear annihilation and an horrific future in which machines with artificial intelligence attempt to destroy humanity. Movie-goers embraced both women with gusto, as if the sight of women saving the world in popular films was perfectly commonplace. However, the point is that when Ripley made her debut, it was anything but commonplace. On the contrary, it was entirely revolutionary for women to appear in the heroic roles usually assigned only to men, and it is this revolutionary appropriation – and even revisioning – of masculinity and heroism that I wish to address in this book.

This remarkable phenomenon was repeated again when the film *Buffy the Vampire Slayer* featured yet another fearless female hero saving the world – this time, in the unlikely form of a blonde schoolgirl cheerleader, destined to protect the world from the onslaught of vampires. The film was released in 1992, but enjoyed only moderate success with audiences. This was most likely due to the impressively bad acting of the lead, Kirsty Swanson, as well as the fact that Donald Sutherland seemed visibly embarrassed to even be in the movie – as he commented, "I just couldn't *bring* myself to say I was making a film called *Buffy the Vampire Slayer*" (Kuzui and Whedon 1992). Nevertheless, the movie did attract a cult following, and had sufficient resonance that, five years later, it spawned one of the most successful television series of all time, also titled *Buffy the Vampire Slayer*. As Buffy's creator, Joss Whedon, said: "I saw so many horror movies where there was that blonde girl who would always get herself killed. … I thought it was time she had a chance to take back the night" (Kuzui and Whedon 1992).

Millions of viewers clearly agreed – the television series premiered in 1997, and ran for an impressive seven seasons, to both critical and popular acclaim. In 2001, at the end of the fifth season, Buffy gave her life to save the world, thus apparently ending the entire series – but she had to be resurrected from her grave for two more seasons, due to the overwhelming outcry from her fans. Buffy "died" in May of 2001, but by October of the same year she was once again alive and (literally) kicking.

BUFFY WAS NOT THE ONLY FEMALE HERO TO INVADE HOMES via the small screen. Programmes like *Xena: Warrior Princess* (which premiered in 1995) and *La Femme Nikita* (which premiered in 1997) were also huge successes. Moreover, the trend shows no signs of abating. The year 2006 saw the release of *Heroes*, a new television series and an unexpectedly massive hit, given that it is science fiction. The show features a number of young people with mysterious superpowers. Their mission – as is usual in many science fiction texts – is to save the world. But the important point is that the most important hero of them all – the one who is destined to save the world – is Claire Bennet, an undeniably female, blonde cheerleader! And while this character looks superficially rather demure, she displays a seriousness and quiet courage that entirely befit a hero.

CLEARLY, THE NEW FEMALE HERO HAS BECOME AN enduring part of popular culture. As Hills sums it up:

> Smarter, tougher and better equipped than
> both the traditional heroines of the action
> genre and many of their contemporary male
> counterparts, action heroines are a new
> breed of arse-kicking female protagonists
> in action genre films. Aggressive, heroic and
> transformative characters such as Ripley
> from the *Alien* series, Sarah Connor from
> *Terminator 2: Judgment Day* (James Cameron,
> 1991), Rebecca from *Tank Girl* (Rachel
> Talalay, 1995), Morgan Adams from *Cutthroat
> Island* (Renny Harlan, 1995), both Thelma
> and Louise (Ridley Scott, 1991) all of the
> *Bad Girls* (Jonathan Kaplan, 1994) and, more
> recently, Samantha/Charlie [sic] from *The
> Long Kiss Goodnight* (Renny Harlan, 1996)
> transgress both cinematic genre codes and
> cultural gender codes which position female
> characters as the passive, immobile and

> peripheral characters of Hollywood action
> cinema. ... [T]hese powerfully transgressive
> characters open up interesting questions
> about the fluidity of gendered identities and
> changing popular cinematic representations
> of women ... (Hills 1999: 38)

What has happened is that there has been a vast sea change
in filmic representations of heroes: traditionally always
depicted as men, now they can be women. Hitherto, "action
heroines have been difficult to conceptualize as heroic
female characters ... [because of] the binaristic logic of
... theoretical models" (Hills 1999: 39). As Hills (1999)
points out, even many feminist theorists have been unable
to conceive of female heroes because of the constraints of
such binaristic models. However, some popular filmic texts
in the last three decades appear to be having no problem at
all in conceptualizing heroic female characters. By the same
token, mass audiences are having no problem in accepting
them: "*Alien* and its sequels showed that millions of audience
members 'of both sexes could connect powerfully to the
image of a ... heroine getting sweaty and bloody in brutal
physical combat with a monster'" (Inness 2004: 3). Similarly,
television shows featuring female heroes continue to repeat
endlessly in syndication, and also continue to have active web
sites devoted to them: "Clearly they resonate with fans and
critics hungry for female heroes" (Magoulick 2006: 731).

Thus, it would seem to be a logical deduction that the
rigid gender binary is beginning to break down in the popular
media. In using the phrase "gender binary," I refer to the
social and theoretical systems that insist and even prescribe
that there are two – and only two – genders, and that these

two genders are most usefully defined as being the opposites of one another. Moreover, this system commonly posits the male as the norm, and the female as merely the not-male, the "other," or simply the opposite of the norm. In this book, I examine the breaking down of this concept in recent filmic and television texts, focusing on texts in which women have performed a role previously only performed by men: the role of the hero. In particular, I examine the *Alien* movies and *Terminator 1* and *2*, and television shows such as *Buffy the Vampire Slayer, Xena: Warrior Princess* and *Star Trek Voyager*. My objective is to show that women have been able to take on the role of hero because of important shifts in the way our Western society views or constructs gender. It is also to show that an extremely important shift has taken place in the way in which the archetype of hero is visioned in our culture, as reflected in our popular media.

THERE ARE CRITICS WHO DISMISS THE APPEARANCE OF female heroes as no more than a transient fashion trend, with no real significance. However, Inness addresses this contingency as follows:

> Do the new styles and behaviors show, as
> Gerard Jones argues, a profound shift in
> the "relationship of women, to power, sex,
> and aggression"? He believes that rather
> than being just the latest fashion trend,
> these images reflect the fact that women
> are challenging the male monopoly of
> power and aggression, a shift that has broad
> ramifications for how gender is constructed.
> (Inness 2004: 5)

I argue that Jones is correct: what we are witnessing is a dynamic change in the formerly rigid control exerted by the gender binary. This dynamic, indeed transgressive, change is reflected by popular filmic texts, which in turn are influencing this dynamic change in the real world. In this book I examine popular filmic texts with a view to unpacking what they reveal about two key, related concepts: female masculinity and the new phenomenon of female heroes. In doing so, I join a number of other commentators who have perceived these films as "texts with social contexts and possible uses in the reconstruction of masculinity and femininity" (McCaughey and King 2001: 3).

It is necessary at this point to clarify what I mean by the term "masculinity" in this analysis. Traditionally, masculinity has meant "of or characteristic of men" and, when applied to a woman, "having qualities considered appropriate to a man" (Barber 1998: 888). However, as Sedgwick (1995) points out, contemporary gender scholars have asserted that masculinity sometimes has nothing to do with men. In short, the term "masculinity" is not necessarily to be associated with a person who has a biologically male body; the attributes that we dub "masculinity" may be expressed by all kinds of bodies. Indeed, it may be argued that there is a political agenda underlying the attempt to restrict the power implicit in masculinity to men, and therefore, as Halberstam argues, "female masculinities are rejected in order that male masculinity may appear to be the real thing" (1998: 1). The political and sociological purpose of the attempt to restrict masculinity to men will be explored further in Chapter 2. At this point, suffice to say that masculinity need not necessarily be restricted purely to people born in male bodies. As Halberstam has pointed out, female masculinity has been frequently manifested in all societies: "what we understand as heroic masculinity has been produced by and across both male and female bodies" (1998: 2). Once that point is accepted, masculinity becomes more open, so that Berger and his co-editors can ask: "Can the univalent notion of masculinity be replaced by the idea of multiple masculinities in which rigid boundaries of sexual and gender representation are blurred and even redrawn?" (Berger, Wallis, and Watson 1995: 3).

I argue that the notion of multiple masculinities can and should be embraced, and moreover that the notion of multiple masculinities seems to be reflective of the realities currently evident in the Western popular media, such as the filmic texts I discuss. Once this notion is accepted, "female masculinity" ceases to be an oxymoron. It becomes an authentic expression of gender, rather than an inauthentic copy of male masculinity.

After all, as has been argued by Butler and other theorists, "female masculinity" is as real – or as unreal – as "male masculinity." Indeed, Butler sets out to oppose "... those regimes of truth that stipulated that certain kinds of gendered expression were ... false or derivative, and others, true and original" (1990: viii). Butler succeeds in this aim, constructing a provocative theory of gender as performativity, in terms of which we may perceive all gender performances as equally authentic or inauthentic. In other words, a male who performs masculinity, or who assumes a masculine position in society, is no more "authentically masculine" than is a female who performs masculinity.

FEMALE MASCULINITY IS BECOMING INCREASINGLY EVIDENT in social life as well as in media representations. Moreover, it is expressed in many different ways.

For example, Noble suggests that: "Female masculinity references a range of subject positions – drag king, butch, female to male (FTM), transman (both operative and non-operative), trans-gendered man, stone butch[4] ..." (Noble 2004: xi). Noble does not clarify precisely what she means by masculinity, or by female masculinity, but it seems clear from the subject positions she mentions that she associates masculinity with physical appearance. This inference may be made because all of these subject positions she names have one thing in common: they all present an appearance that is more commonly associated with biologically male persons – to the point that many of them will be frequently "read" as male.

I suggest that this association is erroneous, positing as it does that "female masculinity" consists merely or primarily in *appearing* male. Noble refers to misleading articulations, such as the linkages that the men in Plato's cave allegory made between the sounds of voices and the shadows cast on the back of the cave (Hamilton and Cairns 1961). I argue that Noble makes a similarly false articulation by limiting masculinity to those who present an *appearance* of maleness.

People have a wide variety of choices in terms of behavior. They do not necessarily have to behave according to the way they appear. Hence, masculinity may be presented by appearance or by behaviors. People of either gender may present in a masculine manner, and they may or may not also exhibit traditionally masculine behaviors. In any of these possible combinations, they could be described as masculine. However, in this book I am concerned primarily with behaviors, and accordingly I suggest that masculinity references a set of behaviors and ways of thinking. Thus, I propose the following definition of female masculinity:

> Female masculinity is a particular expression
> or performance of masculinity, an expression
> or performance that is entirely authentic,
> and that consists in female-bodied persons
> engaging in ways of thought and behavior
> that have traditionally been considered
> masculine, such as claiming the right to
> authority, or displaying strength, courage,
> assertiveness, leadership, physicality (and
> sometimes violence), and very often heroism.
> Thus, female masculinity consists in female-
> bodied persons expressing characteristics
> that have traditionally been considered
> quintessentially masculine.

My definition of female masculinity emphasizes masculine characteristics that may be displayed in a person who does not appear in any way male. In popular culture, this would include characters such as Sarah Connor in the *Terminator* series, who – while not being in any danger of being mistaken for a fashion model – is nevertheless extremely unlikely to be mistaken for a man. Similarly, television's Buffy the Vampire Slayer, played by the petite, feminine-appearing Sarah Michelle Geller, could never be mistaken for a man – yet she is the unquestioned leader of all her peers, exhibiting a growing right to power and authority as the series progresses, being courageous and strong to a fault, and moreover regularly saving the world from imminent apocalypse. She has all the strengths of the archetypal masculine hero, regardless of the fact that she does not look remotely like a man.

As Inness expresses it, "Like Buffy, Barb Wire, and Sarah Pezzini, many of the new tough women are attractive, feminine, and heterosexually appealing but they also challenge the patriarchal social structure by defending women and acting against the men who threaten them" (Inness 2004: 14).

In short, clothes do *not* make the man – and neither do short haircuts or androgynous features. Rather, it is what the person thinks and does that denote masculinity. My definition broadens the concept of masculinity in a way that is potentially more subversive of the current male-dominated patriarchy than a narrower, appearance-linked definition, as it opens a doorway for women who prefer to conform physically to social mores to lay claim nevertheless to the authoritativeness and power that has traditionally been the domain of men.

IT IS NOTEWORTHY THAT SUCH A DEFINITION HAS BEEN implicitly assumed in other cultures. For example, Ramet (1996: 2-3) points out that "among the Plains tribes in the nineteenth century ... cross-gender status did not necessarily involve cross-dressing, and some cross-gender females continued to wear female clothes even though they were engaged exclusively in male tasks and took wives to take care of household tasks associated with females." At the same time, I acknowledge that female masculinity is most commonly associated with women who "look like men". However, there are examples of such women who eschew traditionally masculine behaviors and attitudes, while conversely there are many examples of feminine-looking women with masculine ways of thinking and behaviors.[5] The key point, however, is that *female masculinity pertains to what a woman does, not what she looks like.* As Jodie Foster expressed it, talking about her role in 1991's *The Silence of the Lambs*:

> I think there's something very important
> about having a woman hero who's a true
> woman hero, in the most archetypal sense
> of the word, and yet doesn't have to clothe
> herself in men's clothing. She's not six-foot-
> two; she doesn't kill the dragon by being
> mightier. She actually does it because of her
> instinct, because of her brain …. And that's
> a real side of female heroism that should
> be applauded and should be respected.
> … Clarice is a real female hero, not a bad
> imitation of a male hero. (McCaughey and
> King 2001: 14, my emphasis)

This brings me to the other key concept in this book, namely, that of the new female hero. As noted above in this chapter, there are many different expressions of female masculinity, both in real life and in media representations. However, I am concerned here with only one particular kind of female masculinity: the kind that is performed by female heroes who have appeared in recent popular filmic texts. Accordingly, in this book I examine the ways in which recent filmic texts have portrayed transgressive gender behaviors – and specifically the ways in which they have portrayed female masculinity. In so doing, I will argue, these texts have created an entirely new kind of hero, the *new female hero*.

This is a major change because heroes traditionally have been male. As Le Guin puts it, "In our hero-tales of the Western world, heroism has been gendered: The hero is a man. Women may be good and brave, but with rare exceptions … women are not heroes" (1993: 5). Le Guin recalls that there came a point when she looked back over her own opus, and realized that she had unthinkingly complied with the male-centered archetypes of the collective Western consciousness. Yet as she points out:

> These are Jungian archetypes; without
> devaluing Jung's immensely useful concept
> of the archetype as an essential mode
> of thought, we might be aware that the
> archetypes he identified are mind forms of
> the Western European psyche as perceived
> by a man. (Le Guin 1993: 5-6)

Le Guin then deals with the immensely important conceptual distinction between the terms "hero" and "heroine." As she explains:

> In *The Tombs of Atuan*, Arha/Tenar is not
> a hero, she is a heroine. The two English
> words are enormously different in their
> implications and value; they are indeed
> a wonderful exhibition of how gender
> expectations are reflected/created by
> linguistic usage. (Le Guin 1993: 9)

Russ (1995: 81-82) expands on the distinction between "hero" and "heroine," making the crucial point that the terms are anything but coterminous:

> Culture is male. Our literary myths are for
> heroes, not heroines. ... [I]t is impossible
> to write a conventional success story with
> a heroine, for success in male terms is

> failure for a woman, a "fact" movies, books,
> and television plays have been earnestly
> proving to us for decades. Nor is the hard-
> drinking, hard-fighting hero imagined as
> female ... With one or two exceptions ...
> all sub-literary genres are closed to the
> heroine ... For the heroine the conflict
> between success and sexuality is itself
> the issue, and the duality is absolute. The
> woman who becomes hard and unfeminine,
> who competes with men, finally becomes
> ... a Bitch. Women in twentieth-century
> American literature seem ... limited to either
> Devourer/Bitches or Maiden/Victims.

The point that emerges from this is that while the term "heroine" should mean a hero who is a female, the fact is that this is a contradiction in terms, given the gender binary that prescribes that women are by definition not heroic (for heroism is associated with masculinity, which is presumed to be unavailable to authentic women). Thus, the term "heroine" is a term fraught with inherent contradictions: it is not a woman who is a brave, assertive leader who saves the world – rather, it is a woman with serious problems who is unlikely to find fulfillment and happiness as a woman. Accordingly for a man, being a hero may be perceived as the ultimate fulfillment of his masculine destiny, while for a woman, being a heroine implies subversion of her feminine destiny. It is thus clear that what is required in order for women to truly don the hero's cape is a revisioning of the hero archetype, so that we may have the vision of *a female hero, rather than a heroine.*

Le Guin (1993: 9) concedes that she "had not yet thought what a female hero might be," and therefore set herself the task of trying to imagine what a female hero might be. The outcome of this was her depiction of a female hero in *Tehanu*, the fourth book in the *Earthsea* trilogy. This achievement caused Le Guin to recall with satisfaction that in "Adrienne Rich's invaluable word, I had 'revisioned' *Earthsea*" (Le Guin 1993: 12). She acknowledges that this was due to the influence of feminism, and concedes further: "When the world turns over, you can't go on thinking upside down. What was innocence is now irresponsibility. *Vision must be revisioned*" (Le Guin 1993: 12, my emphasis).

T HE WORLD HAS CONTINUED TO BE TURNED UPSIDE down since Le Guin delivered her *Earthsea Revisioned* address at Oxford University in 1992. So it is that we can now look back on many examples of film-makers setting out to think what a female hero might be, and portraying their visions in films – and in the process entirely revisioning the hero archetype. Le Guin notes that the literary tradition which portrayed heroes only as men was based on a myth that perceived "men as independently real and women ... only as non-men" (1993: 16). However, she argues that "thanks to the revisioning of gender called feminism, we can see the myth as a myth: a construct, which may be changed; an idea which may be rethought, made more true, more honest" (Le Guin 1993: 17). This, I argue, is what recent filmic texts have done – they have revisioned gender, and thus changed the myth of heroism into a more honest (and more inclusive) myth, in that for the first time, women are also allowed to be heroes. Le Guin sees this kind of revisioning as profoundly transformative:

> The deepest foundation of the order of
> oppression is gendering, which names the
> male normal, dominant, active, and the
> female other, subject, passive. To begin to
> imagine freedom, the myths of gender, like
> the myths of race, have to be explored and
> discarded. My fiction does that by these
> troubling and ugly embodiments. (Le Guin
> 1993: 24)

Similarly, recent filmic texts have explored and discarded
the myth that only men may be heroes. In doing so, they
have begun to imagine freedom from the myths of gender,
in that they have allowed female characters to take on the
masculine characteristics I noted above in my definition of
masculinity: *claiming the right to authority, or displaying strength,
courage, assertiveness, leadership, physicality (and sometimes violence),
and very often heroism.*

Of all of these masculine characteristics, perhaps the
most surprising is *physicality (and sometimes violence)*, for this has
traditionally been associated only with males. But now:

> One of the hallmarks of the new heroine is
> her ability to utilize her body to effectively
> kick, punch, maim, and kill others,
> particularly men. This kind of physicality
> inherently involves violence. To the extent
> that violence is considered integral to the
> construction of masculinity, and hence
> antithetical to femininity, the existence
> of (violent) heroines is in and of itself
> transgressive. (Tung 2004: 101)

Certainly violence is frequently a component in the construction of masculinity. Moreover it is displayed by almost all of the heroes in this book. These are not women who react to a crisis by swooning until someone passes the smelling salts, or by screaming hysterically in corners. Rather, they react with physicality and even violence, if it is the appropriately heroic way to react in order to save the day (or the girl, or the world – and even, surprisingly often, the boy).

This physicality and even violence is undeniably transgressive. However, this is not the only transgressive aspect of female heroes. The kind of masculinity performed by the new female heroes goes *further* in deconstructing the myth of the gender binary, in that these female heroes do not *only* display characteristics traditionally reserved for men. They go further than this, for they also incorporate traditionally feminine behaviors and characteristics into their heroic activities, thus broadening the hero archetype in a way that is transformative, transgressive and liberatory. For example, as argued by Hills (1999), Ripley (in the *Alien* films) is not simply a female version of the male hero. Rather, she is all that and *more*. She displays an

> ... ability to adapt to the new: to negotiate
> change. Ripley illustrates the importance
> of creative thinking in response to the new
> signs which occur in her environment, a
> willingness to experiment with new modes
> of being and the ability to transform herself
> in the process. (Hills 1999: 40)

Moreover, Hills (1999) dismisses critic Judith Newton, who has attempted to reduce Ripley to a hero who is lacking "radical thrust" because she sometimes exhibits "feminine" behaviors, as for example when she rescues a cat at the end of *Alien* (Scott 1979), or when she becomes obsessed with rescuing a little girl called Newt in *Aliens* (Cameron 1986). I would agreed with Newton, and suggest that the hero archetype attains an even more radical thrust when it dares to embrace aspects of its supposed opposite, that is, aspects of the feminine archetype. Similarly, some critics, such as Ros Jennings, have argued that because Ripley appears stripped to her underwear in the final sequence of *Alien*, she cannot be perceived as a hero. However, Hills (1999) recalls and rebuts Jennings's argument:

> By rendering her available to male voyeurism, Scott's control of filming in the final scene ensures that in addition to the so-called masculine traits of bravery, technical ability and so on – she now signifies a wholly intelligible form of femininity. Far from celebrating Ripley's access to both masculine and feminine qualities, Jennings reads Ripley's "femininity" as disqualifying her as a hero. Because Ripley is shown to be vulnerable as well as brave she can be only a token hero. (Hills 1999: 42-43)

However, it is suggested that this misses the point, as it is based on binaristic, either/or thinking. Hills (1999) points out that, contrary to Newton's or Jennings's dismissal of Ripley's status as action heroine, the fact that Ripley is so multi-faceted is precisely what makes her a female action hero:

> … as Yvonne Tasker has argued, this play
> of vulnerability and strength is characteristic
> of the action hero/heroine. Indeed, it is
> during her final confrontation with the
> alien that Ripley is most visibly an action
> heroine for, stripped down to her underwear,
> she presents audiences with an image of a
> female character who is both victim and her
> own rescuer: *a character which breaks down the
> hierarchical division of active-male/passive-female.*
> Whilst shots of Ripley in her bikini briefs
> certainly eroticize her image, her actions
> supply a strong counter-narrative. In other
> words, not only does Ripley put on a space
> suit before doing battle with the alien, she
> also single-handedly defeats it. (Hills 1999:
> 43, my emphasis)

In short, Ripley incorporates in one body traditionally male and female attributes, and this does not disqualify her from being a hero. On the contrary, it positions her as an entirely different kind of hero, in that she *at once lays claim to a status usually inhabited only by men, and at the same time transforms and enriches this heroic status by broadening it to include some traditionally female attributes.* As I will show, a similar transformative process can be seen in other female action heroes, both on the small and the large screens. For example, as has been powerfully argued by Ross (2004), the heroes in *Buffy the Vampire Slayer* and *Xena: Warrior Princess* "push the limits of what it means to be a hero" (231). They are flexible, and they talk with their woman friends in order "to understand how their experiences are rooted in patriarchy, so that they may take action to improve their lives as women" (232). This applies to both the titular heroes and their women friends. Thus, in stark contrast to the archetypal isolated male action hero, these women construct their heroism within a community, and are not so much heroes *for* other women as heroes *with* them: "The lead characters must be strong enough psychologically and emotionally to *change their approaches to being heroic*; they learn that the toughest hero is a flexible one who relies on others" (Ross 2004: 233, my emphasis). In similar vein, Samantha/Charly in *The Long Kiss Goodnight* (Harlin 1996) ultimately is able to incorporate her maternal love for her daughter Caitlin; while Ripley combines tough heroism with protective, probably maternal feeling for little Newt in *Aliens* (Cameron 1986); and Sarah Connor in *Terminator 1* and *2* (Cameron 1984 and 1991) is motivated by her desire to save the world, as well as by her powerful love for her son, which motivates her to want to save him from his destiny of spending his adulthood fighting a doomed battle against the machines.

Thus, the female hero broadens the category of hero by combining female masculinity with traditionally feminine characteristics, such as the maternal instinct, flexibility, sharing and a talent for and enjoyment of communication. Due to the transformative nature of the depiction of female heroes in recent filmic texts, I will make reference to Gilles Deleuze's notion of bodies as transgressive and transformative to explore the development of female hero characters such as Ripley, Sarah Connor, Xena and Buffy.

I N SUM, IN THIS BOOK I EXAMINE A SELECT FEW, POPULAR FILMS and television shows released since 1979. All of these texts feature women who display female masculinity, specifically in their roles as action heroes. I argue that these depictions constitute an ongoing transgressive and liberatory attack on the gender binary, and that they are forging new ways of being a woman, new ways of being masculine, and new ways of being a hero, in the popular consciousness. This is creating a dynamically altered social milieu, in which growing girls and grown women are exposed to alternative, transgressive and ultimately liberatory ways to perform their own gender. At the same time, it must be borne in mind that these depictions have arisen precisely *because* of shifts in the popular consciousness, specifically what Le Guin refers to as "the revisioning of gender called feminism" (1993: 17). It would seem that media representations of female masculinity both reflect and shape new understandings of gender and gender transgression. As noted by Magoulick, with regard to the television shows of the 1990s which featured strong female heroes:

> Producers of these shows sought to answer women's growing discontent and dismay at their treatment in the media. Significantly, these responses to frustration at the lack of strong roles for women on TV coincided with growing numbers of female viewers with disposable income and spending potential. (2006: 731)

In my analysis, I draw on the insights of feminist and queer theorists, notably Halberstam and Butler. The former provides invaluable insights into female masculinity and the inadequacy of the gender binary, while the latter provides an innovative way of understanding and deconstructing the gender binary. Halberstam's analysis will be used to elucidate the shortcomings and paucity of the rigid gender binary, as well as the political reasons why it exists in the first place. Butler's insights will be used to augment Halberstam's critique that the gender binary, so far from being an inevitable biological identity, is a social construct, possibly even mere performativity. If gender is mere performativity, it follows that we may choose to perform alternative roles. This is precisely what the female action hero demonstrably does. Thus, I argue that the female action hero's masculinity is profoundly important in the social sphere, for it strikes a much-needed blow at the limiting constraints of the gender binary. At the same time, I suggest that the female action hero's masculinity is profoundly important in the fictional sphere, for as I will show, it has enabled a revisioning of the ancient archetype of the hero.

NOTES

1 My idea of the "female hero" draws on notions of heroism in myth, as articulated by Campbell, as well as those of female heroism, as articulated by Carol Pearson and Katherine Pope. Feminist texts have frequently subverted the rigid role division within patriarchy, according to which women "can't" be heroes, as Annis Pratt and Judith Kegan Gardiner mention.

2 Throughout this book, the term "masculinity" is used in a consciously narrow context. It alludes to a select few, supposedly "masculine" characteristics, which will be clearly delineated in the pages below. These are characteristics considered "positive" in the public sphere in general, and in the sphere of the heroic archetype,

in particular. This is not intended to imply that masculinity in general is perceived as static; neither is it intended to imply a valorization of masculinity, and hence of patriarchal power. As is noted by theorists such as Jean Noble, there are in fact multiple masculinities, just as there are multiple femininities. For example, Judith Halberstam's concept of "gender strangeness" emphasizes anomalies and shifts in gender, thus avoiding reinforcing stereotypes associated with each gender. The intent in this book is to focus on specific characteristics that have traditionally been associated with masculinity, without at the same time implying that these embody the essence of a perceived unitary masculinity.

3 "Saving the world" is a common trope in science fiction and fantasy for heroic status.

4 "Stone butch" usually refers to lesbians who do not allow their sexual partners to touch them intimately. This is usually perceived as a way in which they negate their own femaleness, thus underlining the butch persona.

5 In addition, it needs to be made clear that female masculinity should not be taken as coterminous with lesbianism. The notion that it is appears to derive from the gender binary which designates two opposite sexes, with each person belonging clearly to one or the other, and needing to pair up with an opposite in order to achieve natural completion. From this notion, it is an easy step to imagine that all masculine-identified or masculine-acting people must necessarily choose female persons as a love or desire object. While it is true that female masculinity and lesbianism quite frequently do co-exist in the same person, the important point is that neither *necessarily* implies the other. As noted by Noble, "female masculinity has erroneously become coterminous with ontological 'lesbianism' (not all female masculinities are lesbian; not all lesbians are masculine …)" (2004: xii). In this respect, it is notable that most of the masculine female characters in this book are heterosexual.

CHAPTER 2

GENDER THEORY AND
FEMALE ACTION HEROES

As discussed in Chapter 1, there has been a major shift in possible ways of envisioning women, so that it is now possible to see women as action heroes with "masculine" behavioral traits, rather than as "non-men" cowering in the corner, emitting piercing shrieks while waiting to be rescued (by a man, of course). Moreover, the new female action heroes who now grace our popular entertainment screens are not just female versions of the traditional masculine hero: on the contrary, they embody an entirely different kind of hero, for they not only lay claim to the heroic status previously enjoyed only by men, but also transform and enrich the traditional heroic role by broadening it to include some traditionally female attributes, such as the maternal instinct, flexibility, sharing, and a talent for and enjoyment of communication. Thus, concomitant with what Le Guin calls "the revisioning of gender called feminism" (1993: 17), in recent films and television programmes there has been a *revisioning of the action hero*. The question must be asked: how has this revisioning been possible?

After all, as pointed out by Fausto-Sterling (2000: 3), homosexuals did not exist in ancient Greece – there were merely married, heterosexual male citizens who sometimes had sex with boys or men, when they felt like it. Only in the modern world, where the concept of "a homosexual" exists, is it possible for a person to imagine her- or himself as "a homosexual", with the accompanying psychosocial identity and way of loving. Similarly, it is now possible for us to perceive women as capable of being action heroes with some masculine behavioral traits, precisely because there has been a profound shift in how we are able to envision the concept of "woman." Indeed, as Scott points out, poststructuralist theory enables us to "articulate alternative ways of thinking about (and thus acting upon) gender without either simply reversing the old hierarchies or confirming them" (2003: 378). In order to see how we have reached this point, it is helpful to review some of the pertinent history of gender theory, and the way in which literary texts of specific time periods have reflected the contemporaneous ways of framing gender identity. This should shed light on how we have evolved to the point where the popular consciousness, the popular media, and also gender theory are able to conceive of this revisioning of the traditional action hero, and can comfortably accommodate, and even enjoy, the sight of a "masculine" woman taking on a role previously available only to men – that of the action hero.

U P UNTIL AROUND THE MIDDLE OF THE TWENTIETH century, it was almost universally believed[1] that gender[2] is assigned by biology, so that biological maleness inevitably implies sociological masculinity, and biological femaleness inevitably implies sociological femininity.[3] It was also widely assumed that all infants are born clearly and indisputably either one sex or the other, and that once they reach sexual maturity they will inevitably and universally wish to choose a sexual partner of the opposite sex. This group of assumptions is sometimes referred to as biological essentialism, and is built upon a view of the world that reduces most of human behavior to genetics (Fausto-Sterling 2000: 233-255). Reduced to its most ludicrous level, this argument means that XX sex chromosomes invariably result in the wearing of pink dresses. Or, in the context of my argument, XX sex chromosomes result in cowering in corners, screaming, while someone with XY sex chromosomes boldly confronts the monster *du jour* and uses his strength to dispatch it, thus saving said cowering XX victim (who seems in fact to be doubly victimized, both by the monster and by her fatally flawed sex chromosomes).

As simplistic as it sounds when thus crudely expressed, I nevertheless contend that the widespread and uncritical acceptance of biological essentialism is reflected in a wealth of literature, which implicitly affirms biological essentialism. Granted, there are exceptions, some dating back many centuries. Shakespeare himself was fond of a bit of gender bending, as seen for example in *Twelfth Night* – although his characters invariably ended up reverting to "gender-appropriate" clothing and behavior, and in heterosexual relationships (Olivia's infatuation with Viola notwithstanding). Even Jane Austen, that doyenne of impeccable Regency England mores, was not above featuring the odd tomboy character, such as Catherine Morland in *Northanger Abbey*, whose childhood is described as follows:

> Catherine … had a thin awkward figure,
> a sallow skin without colour, dark lank
> hair, and strong features; so much for
> her person, and not less unpropitious for
> heroism seemed her mind. She was fond
> of all boys' plays, and greatly preferred
> cricket, not merely to dolls, but to the more
> heroic enjoyments of infancy, nursing a
> dormouse, feeding a canary-bird or watering
> a rose-bush. Indeed she had no taste for
> gardens, and if she gathered flowers at all, it
> was chiefly for the pleasure of mischief, at
> least so it was conjectured from her always
> preferring those which she was forbidden to
> take. Such were her propensities; her abilities
> were quite as extraordinary. (Austen, 1996: 1)

Thus, Catherine Morland starts off her life displaying a penchant for activities deemed more appropriate to those born biologically male. However, it is notable that the girl's propensities are described as "extraordinary." Moreover, she quickly recovers from her odd propensities, and thereafter focuses on attending balls and meeting men. In general, Austen does not appear to question the gender binary as the basis of the social system in which she lived. In fact, Auerbach (2001) goes so far as to assert that in some of Austen's books the only thing that animates women's lives is the presence of the "opposite" sex. As she puts it, a "collective waiting for the door to open and a Pygmalion to bring life into limbo defines the female world of *Pride and Prejudice*" (327). Hence, Austen appears to give Catherine Morland "inappropriately" masculine characteristics not to challenge biological essentialism, but merely to position her as different, thus laying the foundation for her later inappropriately active imagination.

Notwithstanding exceptions such as those just noted, there can be no question but that the vast bulk of Western literature features characters who are unequivocally either feminine women or masculine men, and who are equally unequivocally heterosexual. This was based on a widespread and largely uncritical acceptance of biological essentialism, but the main problem with biological essentialism is that it offers no explanation for those who do not fit into either of the two defined categories (i.e. feminine women or masculine men). How are masculine women to be explained, or feminine men, or homosexuals? If biology prescribes behaviors and sexuality, how is it possible that anyone can be an exception?

The solution to this apparent contradiction turned out to be elegantly simple, and is well summarized by Fausto-Sterling:

> ... definitions of homo- and heterosexuality were built on a two-sex model of masculinity and femininity. The Victorians, for example, contrasted the sexually aggressive male with the sexually indifferent female. But this created a mystery. If only men felt active desire, how could two women develop a mutual sexual interest? The answer: one of the women had to be an invert, someone with markedly masculine attributes. This same logic applied to male homosexuals, who were seen as more effeminate than heterosexual men. (Fausto-Sterling, 2000: 14)

In short, masculine women, feminine men, and homosexuals were simply exceptions who proved the rule, inversions or opposites of the norm, and the reasons for their deviations from the rules were likely to be medical. For example, Kraft-Ebbing's *Psychopathia Sexualis* (1892) sees homosexuality as an inversion arising from anomalies in the womb, while Havelock Ellis's *Sexual Inversion* (1898) argues that homosexuality (i.e. the inversion of the sex object) is a "congenital (and thus involuntary) physiological abnormality" (Somerville 248). Ironically, while Kraft-Ebbing's and Ellis's theories attempted to excuse or explain homosexual object-choice and hence reduce the pariah status of homosexuals, by pathologizing homosexuality they ultimately achieved precisely the opposite. As Halberstam explains, "there was a larger cultural imperative at work, namely, the desire to reduce sexuality to binary systems of gender difference" (1998: 76). Moreover, as is argued by Foucault, what was happening was that the discourse of sexuality was being transformed into a medical discourse (Foucault 1990: 51-74).

ONCE SEXUALITY WAS TRANSFORMED INTO A MEDICAL discourse, it was but a brief step for non-mainstream manifestations of gender or sexuality to be depicted as pathological. For example, Riviere's well-known article on the subject of womanliness as a masquerade clearly depicts female masculinity as pathological. She refers to masculine women as "women who, while mainly heterosexual in their development, plainly display strong features of the other sex" (Riviere 1929: 1). Going further, she notes that "Not long ago intellectual pursuits for women were associated almost exclusively with an overtly masculine type of woman, who in pronounced cases made no secret of her wish or claim to be a man. This has now changed" (Riviere 1929: 36). She suggests an interesting theory to account for this change – she believes these intellectual women now *masquerade* as womanly. She accordingly attempts to "show that women who wish for masculinity may put on a mask of womanliness to avert anxiety and the retribution feared from men" (Riviere 1929: 36). She appears to base this analysis on her Freudian assumptions. For example, she refers to one woman who alternates between intellectual (and hence, in her terms, "masculine" behavior) and flirtatious (and hence, in her terms, "feminine" behavior) as having an unresolved Oedipal conflict with her mother (Riviere 1929: 37).

I would argue that the key mistake Riviere makes is that she assumes that laying claim to masculine attributes indicates that a woman actually wishes to *be* a man (and thus, in her view, has a psychopathology). For example, she uses the concepts as synonyms, as in "homosexual women who … wish for 'recognition' of their masculinity from men and claim to be the equals of men, *or in other words, to be men themselves*" (Riviere 1929: 2, my emphasis). While this may sometimes be true, one of my key arguments is that usually, this is *not* the case. On the contrary, I would argue that it is more common for women who wish to lay claim to masculine attributes to have no wish at all to be a man.[4]

Of course, Riviere was writing in a different time and place, and it is possible that her theory that masculine women masquerade as womanly women to escape danger has some truth to it. As she put it, "Womanliness therefore could be assumed and worn as a mask, both to hide the possession of masculinity and to avert the reprisals expected if she was found to possess it" (Riviere 1929: 3). This foreshadows Butler's theory of gender as performativity, as expressed in

1990 in her ground-breaking book, *Gender Trouble: Feminism and the Subversion of Identity*. However, Riviere's emphasis on Freudian-defined pathologies appears to make her blind to the intensely sociological motivations for the behaviors she documents. In effect, she refers to women who have strong competencies in activities that have been arbitrarily defined as appropriate only to men – such as fixing a sink. She then comments on the fact that such women hide these abilities, or compensate for them with excessively "feminine" behaviors, and comes up with explanations such as an oedipal complex that arose during the oral-biting sadistic stage (Riviere 1939: 41). In a world where women have throughout history been beaten, raped, tortured, burned alive and murdered for displaying behaviors that men have decreed are appropriate only for men, I would argue that it is far more likely that these women adopted a "masquerade of femininity" due to well-founded fear and a desire for self-preservation, rather than because of lingering problems with transitioning from a desire to bite off the mother's nipple, to a desire to bite off the father's penis (Freeman and Freeman 1992).

AS SELF-EVIDENT AS SOCIAL PRESSURES NOW SEEM TO many of us, nevertheless pathological, psychological or medical discourses tended to dominate thinking about unusual expressions of gender for much of the twentieth century. For example, I believe that this kind of thinking is clearly portrayed in Radclyffe Hall's *Well of Loneliness*, published in 1928. The protagonist, Stephen Gordon, is an entirely masculine woman – much like the author who created her. As Hall wrote in a letter in 1934 to Evguenia Souline, "it may be that being myself a 'misfit,' for as you know beloved, I am a born invert, it may be that I am a writer of 'misfits' in one form or another" (Hall 1997: 23). Accordingly, Stephen's homosexuality is depicted as flowing directly from her inverted nature – she thinks "like a man," and therefore must surely desire women. The fact that her difference is an aberration of nature is emphasized by the fact that even her body is more masculine than feminine, with broad shoulders and slim hips. Her thighs have a "strong, lean line," and her breasts are "slight and compact" (Hall 1974: 321).

The lover Stephen takes, Mary Llewellyn, is portrayed as "normal," in that she falls in love with the masculine gender expression of Stephen, rather than with Stephen's biological femaleness. Hall clearly perceived homosexuals as "inverts" – created by nature, and therefore not morally culpable, but suffering greatly due to being essentially the opposite of normal in terms of gender identity. Tellingly, Stephen first discovers her lesbianism not because she is attracted to a woman, but rather because of her repulsion at the advances of her male friend, Martin. When Martin proposes to her, she responds with the kind of horror a heterosexual man of her time would have experienced if proposed to by another man:

> She was staring at him with a kind of dumb horror, staring at his eyes that were clouded by desire, while gradually over her colourless face there was spreading an expression of the deepest revulsion – terror and repulsion he saw on her face, and something else too, a look as of outrage. … But what was she? Her thoughts, slipping back to her childhood, would find many things in her

> past that perplexed her. She had never been
> quite like the other children, she had always
> been trying to be someone else – that was
> why she had dressed herself up as young
> Nelson. ... In those days she had wanted to
> be a boy – had that been the meaning of the
> pitiful young Nelson? And what about now?
> She had wanted Martin to treat her as a man,
> had expected it of him ... .
> (Hall 1974: 98, 100)

In short, Stephen's lesbianism is not really lesbianism at all. The character Stephen is male in all but body, and it is therefore natural for him to desire women – and to be repulsed by the desire of men. The gender identity of this character is "inverted," and is entirely male despite a female body. On this reading, this is not a book about lesbianism at all, but rather about transgenderism.[5] However, Hall's implicit rationale, that is that lesbianism stems from an inversion of biological gender traits, ignores the reality of feminine lesbians, and also of course fits neatly within the constraints of the gender binary and compulsory heterosexuality,[6] which are built upon an acceptance of biological essentialism. Today, with the benefit of the insights of queer theorists, Hall might be more able to conceive of the naturalness and authenticity of being a masculine woman.[7] But in her time, with no alternatives, she had no choice but to see herself as one cursed by nature to be an "invert:"

> ["Normal" people] sleep the sleep of the
> so-called just and righteous. When they wake
> it will be to persecute those who, through

> no fault of their own, have been set apart
> from the day of their birth, deprived of all
> sympathy, all understanding. (Hall 1974: 389)

UNDERLYING SUCH DESPAIR IS BIOLOGICAL ESSENTIALISM, and the associated pathologizing of those who deviate from the norm. Time fortunately went on, and eventually some people began to question the relationship between biological sex and gender – with some even beginning to perceive the latter as primarily a social expression, a group of behaviors adopted because they conform to social expectations. In 1949, Simone de Beauvoir famously wrote that:

> One is not born, but rather becomes, a
> woman. No biological, psychological, or
> economic fate determines the figure that
> the human female presents in society; it is
> civilization as a whole that produces this
> creature, intermediate between male and
> eunuch which is described as feminine. (De
> Beauvoir 1974: 281)

This existentialist statement may be perceived as an important part of the beginning of a move away from biological essentialism, towards an understanding of gender as a social construct. Naturally, given the fact that it is impossible to tell where nature leaves off and nurture begins in human beings, as (obviously and fortunately) we cannot experiment with human beings, fierce debate ensued between biological essentialists who continued to maintain that sex and gender were indivisible, and those who thought it was possible to separate sex and gender. Writing in 2000, Fausto-Sterling summarized this debate as follows:

> Over the last few decades, the relation between the *social expression* of masculinity and femininity and their *physical underpinnings* has been hotly debated in scientific and social arenas. In 1972 the sexologists John Money and Anke Ehrhardt popularized the idea that sex and gender are separate categories. *Sex*, they argued, refers to physical attributes and is anatomically and physiologically determined. *Gender* they saw as a psychological transformation of the self – the internal conviction that one is either male or female (gender identity) and the behavioural expressions of that conviction. (Fausto-Sterling 2000: 3)

Fausto-Sterling points out that Money's distinction between gender and sex basically posited the physical as "sex" and the mental as "gender" (Fausto-Sterling 1999). She also makes the important point that the notion of sex as an artefact of biology and gender as an artefact of society was echoed by second-wave feminists in the 1970s, who believed that social institutions are responsible for the gender differences so frequently perceived between women and men, and moreover that these differences are intentionally promoted, as they perpetuate male dominance (Fausto-Sterling 2000: 3-4). Fausto-Sterling points out that these feminists, seemingly with little knowledge of Money's work, reinvented the term "gender" in a way that was somewhat different from his usage. In essence, the emphasis in the definition of "gender" moved from the "mental" to the role of culture (Fausto-Sterling 1999). While it is impossible entirely to separate sex and gender, because "to a great extent our bodies' physical appearance (i.e. their physical sex) locates us in our gendered culture," the distinction between the two is nevertheless a conceptually useful one (Fausto-Sterling 1999: 53). As Scott puts it:

> Gender seems to have become a particularly useful word as studies of sex and sexuality have proliferated, for it offers a way of differentiating sexual practice from the social roles assigned to women and men ... . The use of gender emphasises an entire system of relationships that may include sex, but is not directly determined by sex nor directly determining of sexuality. (1998: 32)

It was also a politically useful distinction, as Fausto-Sterling points out:

> This definitional move had a very specific set of political objectives – to make more flexible those behavioral traits and social roles that had traditionally been tied to the body. This move to separate culture from body created room for cultural change with regard to sex roles. (1999: 53)

Thus, the conceptual distinction between sex and gender places the spotlight on the role of culture and society in moulding expressions or performances of gender. As a result, this conceptual move may also be seen as paving the path towards the current situation, where "masculine women" are becoming possible. For if sex and gender are at all separable, and the latter is moulded at least in part by culture, rather than by the incontestable domination of the aforementioned scream-favouring XX sex chromosomes, then it becomes conceptually possible for the XX character to emerge from cowering in the corner, and pick up the cudgels along with the XY character. It even becomes possible for the XX character to take on the monster, while the XY character, his biology overwhelmed by some aspect of his environment, cowers screaming in the corner!

THIS CRUCIAL CONCEPTUAL SHIFT MADE POSSIBLE THE groundbreaking work of Butler, who essentially argues that the categories "masculine" and "feminine" are discursively created as binary opposites within a matrix of heterosexual power. She argues that gender is performative, unfolding as a series of performances, with no pre-existing subject. Some believe that Butler goes too far in negating the physical manifestations of gender. For example, Fausto-Sterling for a long time argued that biological markers, such as genitals, are extremely important in defining gender. Fausto-Sterling believed that the reality of gender was far more complex than the gender binary suggests. In 1993 she published "The Five Sexes: Why Male and Female are not Enough," a proposal that our two-sex system should be replaced with a five-sex system. This would have added to the categories of male and female the categories of herms (true hermaphrodites), ferms (female pseudohermaphrodites), and merms (male pseudohermaphrodites) (Fausto-Sterling

2000). Subsequently, however, Fausto-Sterling has modified her thinking somewhat. In a more recent article she quotes psychologist Suzanne J. Kessler, as follows:

> The limitation with Fausto-Sterling's proposal is that … [it] still gives genitals … primary signifying status and ignores the fact that in the everyday world gender attributions are made without access to genital inspection …. What has primacy in everyday life is the gender that is performed, regardless of the flesh's configuration under the clothes. (Fausto-Sterling 2004: 138)

Fausto-Sterling writes that "I now agree with Kessler's assessment. It would be better for intersexuals and their supporters to turn everyone's focus away from genitals" (Fausto-Sterling 2004: 138). In short, as succinctly summarized by Fausto Sterling, "Labelling someone a man or a woman is a social decision. We may use scientific knowledge to help us make the decision, but only our beliefs about gender – not science – can define our sex" (2000: 3). Moreover, I argue that due to this shift towards understanding gender as a social construct, we have reached a point where it is possible to re-envision women as not entirely determined by their XX sex chromosomes, so that it is possible for mainstream audiences to applaud female heroes as they boldly romp across our various entertainment screens.

Just as the traditional gender stereotypes were reflected in literature, so too gender-bending heroines have begun to appear in literature. For example, as early as 1946, Carson McCullers' entirely tomboy protagonist, Frankie Jasmine, looks back at the wise old age of 12 on her previous summers, when she had been "like president or leader" of the children attempting to dig swimming pools in their backyards (McCullers 2006: 53). Isabel Miller features the very masculine lesbian, Sarah Dowling, in her book *Patience and Sarah* – a novel that has enjoyed enduring popularity since it was published in 1969.

Gender-bending hero/heroines have continued to populate fictional writing until the present day. In 1990, Ann-Marie MacDonald's Constance Ledbelly morphs into maleness in the best Shakespearian tradition in *Goodnight Desdemona (Good Morning Juliet)*. In 1992 readers of Rose Tremain's *Sacred Country* met little Mary Ward, standing in a field, thinking: "I have a secret to tell you, dear, and this is it: I am not Mary. That is a mistake. I am not a girl. I'm a boy" (1992: 6). In 1993, Leslie Feinberg's stone butch protagonist, Jess Goldberg, morphs from butch to passing male (with the help of testosterone), and then back to butch, in *Stone Butch Blues*. And in Yann Martel's critically acclaimed novel *Self*, published in 1996, a young man wakes up one day to find that he is a woman, thus becoming a different kind of masculine woman. Sarah Waters's characters, Nancy Astley and Kitty Butler, make a living by being male impersonators in her extremely successful 1998 novel, *Tipping the Velvet* – and Nancy even manages to support herself for a time by working the streets of London as a rent-"boy." Since then, *Tipping the Velvet* was made into a successful BBC television series in 2002, and was released on DVD in the same year. The protagonist in Jeffery Eugenides's novel *Middlesex* (published in same year as *Tipping the Velvet*) Calliope Stephanides, appears to be a woman in terms of both biology and gender expression, but then turns out to be intersexed due to a 5-alpha-reductase deficiency, and becomes Cal, a bearded, heterosexual man.

W HILE SOME NOVELISTS WRITE ABOUT ALL KINDS OF variations of gender expression, others have reflected changing theories of gender and sex in their explorations of the way in which social influences construct gender. For example, Margaret Atwood's *Cat's Eye* (first published in 1988) contains an interesting account of how the protagonist, Elaine, is educated into the gender-role deemed appropriate for her. Social institutions and other girls teach the young girl – and both are hard and unforgiving taskmasters. Elaine's initiation into the rituals of femaleness begins in elementary school. First, she is made to conform by wearing a uniform deemed appropriate for girls – as Elaine says, "You can't wear pants to school, you have to wear skirts" (Atwood 1999: 59). Although Elaine doesn't mention it, we also know that this works both ways – the boys have to wear pants, and cannot wear skirts. In this way, the lesson begins to be drummed in that girls and boys are different. For the girls the prohibition on pants is a highly impractical rule in a cold, snowy climate, forcing Elaine to stuff her skirt down the legs of her snow pants. Next, the lesson is reinforced by separate doors for GIRLS and BOYS, as well as different behaviors – the girls hold hands, the boys do not. This segregation is so important that breaking one of the rules is said to result in being strapped:

> There's a front door which is never used
> by children. At the back are two grandiose
> entranceways ... inscribed in curvy, solemn

> lettering: GIRLS and BOYS. ... we have
> to line up in twos by classrooms, girls in
> one line, boys in another, and file into our
> separate doors. The girls hold hands; the
> boys don't. If you go in the wrong door you
> get the strap, or so everyone says. (Atwood
> 1999: 60)

In this way, the gender binary is taught, and strictly enforced. Elaine, who has hitherto spent most of her time with her brother, reflects on this "educational" process:

> I'm not used to girls, or familiar with their
> customs. I feel awkward around them,
> I don't know what to say. I know the
> unspoken rules of boys, but with girls I
> sense that I am always on the verge of some
> unforeseen, calamitous blunder. (Atwood
> 1999: 62)

Elaine alludes to girls' customs, and boys' rules. This terminology reflects the stereotype that girls and women are socially and emotionally more subtle and duplicitous than are boys and men. Both terms are consistent with the notion of gender as a set of behaviors that is both taught and enforced by social institutions. The baton is then passed to Elaine's peers: she makes friends with Carol, who talks about which boys are in love with her (Carol), and then asks Elaine which boys are in love with her (Elaine). Interest in this matter has never crossed Elaine's mind, but she realizes that she is expected to have an answer, so she replies that she is not sure. In this way, Elaine begins to act like a girl in order to be accepted by the other girls. Very soon, she is editing what she says around girls.

It is quite clear in this text that Elaine is deliberately, consciously choosing to put on a performance that will gain her social acceptance with her new female peers. As she reflects:

> On Saturdays … I play with Carol and Grace. Because it's winter, we play mostly inside. Playing with girls is different and at first I feel strange as I do it, self-conscious, *as if I'm only doing an imitation of a girl.* But I soon get more used to it. (Atwood 1999: 69, my emphasis)

THIS OF COURSE RECALLS JOAN RIVIERE'S DESCRIPTION of femininity as a "masquerade," as well as Butler's theory of gender as performativity. In this book, Elaine is taught how to "masquerade" as a girl, or to "perform" as a girl, by a variety of social institutions – including her school, her sadistic female friends, and of course the church. When she goes to Sunday School, the gender binary enforced by regular school is reinforced – "Our class is all girls" (Atwood 1999: 131). Having shown how the groundwork of the mechanisms of socializing women into a segregated group are laid, *Cat's Eye* goes on to show the extreme damage that women can inflict upon one another, thus making the unfortunate point that there is no universal sisterhood of women, despite all the socialization mechanisms. Indeed, Cordelia inflicts much damage on Elaine, and Elaine's discomfort with her education into gender roles may be seen as presaging this damage.

The damage and pain inherent in such prescriptive roles is also experienced by Alice Munro's protagonist in her short story "Girls and Boys." This unnamed girl is coerced into gender conformity via humiliation – arguably the main method society uses to coerce girls in general into gender conformity, as well as the main method imposed on Atwood's Elaine. Munro's little girl aspires to be like her father, a fox farmer, rather than like her mother, a farmer's wife confined to domestic chores indoors. She is clearly resisting the gender role models offered by her parents. However, her parents and society in general do not allow her to get away with this. Instead, she is humiliated into accepting that she is "only a girl" (Munro 1996: 127). The first time this happens the insult comes from a stranger. The young girl is helping her father with chores in the fox pen:

> One time a feed salesman came down into
> the pens to talk to him and my father said,
> "Like to have you meet my new hired man."
> I turned away and raked furiously, red in the
> face with pleasure.
>
> "Could of fooled me," said the salesman. "I
> thought it was only a girl."
> (Munro 1996: 116)

Yet still the girl perseveres, clearly sensing that the male world is the sphere of importance and power:

> It seemed to me that work in the house was
> endless, dreary, and peculiarly depressing;
> work done out of doors, and in my father's

service, was ritualistically important.
(Munro 1996: 117)

But sadly, her mother undermines her, playing a similar role to that of Elaine's female peers in *Cat's Eye*, coercing the young girl to accept the limitations supposedly imposed on her by biology:

> I wheeled the tank up to the barn, where
> it was kept, and I heard my mother saying,
> "Wait till Laird [the girl's younger brother]
> gets a little bigger, then you'll have a real
> help. … And then I can use her more in the
> house," I heard my mother say. She had a
> dead-quiet, regretful way of talking about me
> that always made me uneasy. "I just get my
> back turned and she runs off. It's not like I
> had a girl in the family at all."
> (Munro 1999: 117)

This passage is experienced as painfully realistic by many female readers. As noted by Friedman, "Though they don't intend to do so, mothers often end up instilling a sense of learned helplessness in girls" (Friedman 1997: 12). Later, the girl finds there has been good reason for her feeling of unease, as she begins to realize the truth:

> I no longer felt safe. It seemed that in the
> minds of the people around me there was
> a steady undercurrent of thought, not to
> be deflected, on this one subject. The word
> *girl* had formerly seemed to me innocent

and unburdened, like the word *child*; now it
appeared that it was no such thing. A girl was
not, as I had supposed, simply what I was;
it was what I had to become. (Munro 1999: 119,
my emphasis)

This realization recalls De Beauvoir's seminal claim,
quoted at length earlier, that "One is not born, but rather
becomes, a woman" (De Beauvoir 1974: 281). Many years
later, Butler would refer to this claim as follows:

If there is something right in Beauvoir's
claim stating that one is not born, but rather
becomes a woman, it follows that woman
itself is a germ in process, a becoming, a
constructing that cannot rightfully be said to
originate or to end. As an ongoing discursive
practice, it is open to intervention and
resignification. Even when gender seems
to congeal into the most reified forms,
the "congealing" is itself an insistent and
insidious practice, sustained and regulated
by various social means. (Quoted in Salih
2002: 45)

BOTH DE BEAUVOIR AND BUTLER THUS SEE GENDER AS A
process – something one *does*, rather than something
one *is*. Where Butler departs from De Beauvoir is
that she takes a further step, by explicitly disengaging the
gender one does from the biological body one is born with.
She denies that there is an inevitable connection between the

two, and that a female body necessarily entails femininity, while a male body necessarily entails masculinity. On the contrary, gender is separate from biology, being merely a cultural construction, and therefore a person with a female body, for example, can choose to perform masculinity (Salih 2002: 46).

It is from this deconstruction and reframing of the concepts that male is equivalent to masculinity, and female is equivalent to femininity, that the possibilities for alternative expressions of gender flow. And it is precisely these alternative or transgressive expressions that have increasingly been embodied in popular media. Indeed, it is apparent that masculine women of all kinds abound in popular media, especially in television and film.

However, for those who might see this as a feminist triumph over the rigid bonds of the gender binary, it is (sadly) a little premature to uncork the champagne. There remains work to be done, for the popular consciousness exhibits an almost schizophrenic split between what it can enjoy in the media and what it will tolerate in its own home. Indeed, if you ask the average person on the street what she or he thinks about female masculinity, you are likely to be met with a look of blank incomprehension at best, or horrified disgust at worst. As pointed out by Halberstam, masculinity is commonly assumed to be possible and desirable within male bodies only: in her words, there appears to be a "collective failure to imagine and ratify the masculinity produced by, for, and within women" (Halberstam 1998: 15). How can the apparent contradiction inherent within this collective failure of imagination be explained? If "masculine" and "feminine" were discursively created as binary opposites (Butler 1990: viii), and if this discourse has now been enriched and broadened in our entertainment media, why do so many people cling stubbornly to a discourse which is demonstrably redundant? Moreover, why is it impossible for the statement "She's a masculine woman" to be merely a statement of fact? Why is it inconceivable for most that someone might make this statement in a tone of approbation? After all, it is clear that our society respects the attributes traditionally associated with masculinity, such as courage and strength. Therefore, it would seem to make sense to admire these attributes in women as well as in men, and to acknowledge their authenticity, rather than perceive such women as merely sad and imperfect imitations of men.

THE ANSWERS TO ALL OF THE RHETORICAL QUESTIONS above appear to reside in the fact that constructions of the self rely heavily on current political discourses, particularly those that are hegemonic, and that the hegemonic discourse persists in constructing masculinity and the female-bodied as binary opposites. As Haag (1992) expresses it:

> … [I]t is my contention that the relation
> between ideology and experience in and
> of itself has a history: the meaning and
> relative importance of discourses – both
> verbal and symbolic – vary according to
> historical setting. Particularly in the modern
> context, when structures of prohibition
> and repression are heavily dependent on
> objective, scientific formulations of truth –
> the "normal" and the "deviant," for example
> – it is crucial that historians read ideological
> material with an eye to what Foucault labels

> the *micropolitical operations of power: that is, the*
> *extent to which individuals and groups rely on and*
> *inevitably reproduce hegemonic ideologies in their*
> *historically specific conceptions of self — the meaning*
> *of "I" carried to ostensibly private, politically*
> *impervious experiences.* (552, my emphasis)

I contend that this is the mechanism that enables the seemingly schizophrenic conceptual split referred to above. Moreover, I contend that this split must be overcome, if women in general are to escape from the straightjacket constraints of biological essentialism, so that those with XX sex chromosomes can escape from their ignominious plight, "cowering in corners," and emerge to share the limelight of heroism with their XY fellow humans. And it is in this respect that popular texts are so important, for they have presented to the popular view the female action hero, and she has been accepted. Now, however, I suggest that a further step needs to be taken — it is necessary for the *implications* of these portrayals to be more widely recognized and acknowledged. For example, if the general public is able to cheer for Sarah Connor in *Terminator 2*, or for Ripley in *Alien*, then the next step should surely be to acknowledge that female masculinity does in fact exist as an authentic variant of gender expression, and moreover that it is neither abnormal nor pathological. On the contrary, it is just another one of the many, diverse ways in which people are able to perform gender.

The value of these popular texts thus lies in the fact that they provide a stepping stone from which we may hope to progress to female masculinity being honoured in real life, not just on screen. Female action heroes are an important part of the contemporary discourse that frames female subjectivity, and so it follows that if these texts depict female heroes, then over time the dominant political discourse which continues to privilege male masculinity over all else will surely become eroded. Indeed, it will surely become more likely that ordinary women will feel empowered to incorporate the heroism they perceive on their entertainment screens into their constructions of themselves – to don (metaphorically) the hero's cape.

I T MIGHT BE ARGUED THAT RIPLEY AND SARAH CONNOR ARE all very well, but most women do not need to be heroes, neither do they aspire to heroism. However, a key point of my argument is that female action heroes are merely the most extreme representations of the potential liberation that could follow the overcoming of the rigid gender binary that proscribes female masculinity (among other things). The resistance to female masculinity must be overcome, for it stands in the way of true gender equality. As Halberstam explains, the "… widespread indifference to female masculinity … has clearly ideological motivations and has sustained the complex social structures that wed masculinity to maleness and to power and domination" (1998: 2). This is the case because the traits considered masculine are also those that shape and lead our world.

As I stated in my definition of female masculinity, the masculine traits to which I specifically refer are claiming the right to authority, displaying strength, courage, assertiveness, leadership, physicality (and sometimes violence), and very often heroism. While the traits that are considered quintessentially feminine, such as nurturing and sharing, may be very pleasant, they do not build empires, nor do they enable the domination of global commerce. Thus, the defining characteristics of the masculine attributes are that they are empowering in the public sphere.[8] This is precisely why they are valued, and precisely why they are so jealously guarded by the reigning power elite in our society, that is, men. Thus, the reason for the fact that female masculinity is not acknowledged in the hegemonic discourse of our society becomes abundantly clear: as Halberstam explains, this refusal to acknowledge that masculinity can be embodied by women is motivated in part by a desire to hide the fact that masculinity is in fact *constructed* by those men who embody it – it is not simply the natural and inevitable consequence of their male bodies. As Halberstam puts it, "female masculinities are framed as the rejected scraps of dominant masculinity in order that male masculinity may appear to be the real thing" (1998: 1).

It follows that acknowledging the authenticity of female masculinity constitutes a way to begin to challenge, and even deconstruct, the male dominance which still structures our patriarchal society on every level. As Wilchins expresses it: "Rethinking gender … will mean rethinking our politics" (Wilchins 2002: 15). This then is a key point in this argument: in highlighting the revisioning of the traditional concept of heroic masculinity that is embodied in female action heroes in popular culture, I hope to make explicit the liberatory and transformative potential for *all* women of this new blend of all that is best in masculinity and femininity. Moreover, in this book I attempt to contribute to the important project pioneered by Halberstam, namely that of making female masculinity both more visible and acceptable, by focusing on the portrayal of female masculinity in recent filmic texts. I share with Halberstam the premise that "female masculinity is a specific gender with its own cultural history rather than simply a derivative of male masculinity," and I set out to contribute in some small way to the documentation of that cultural history (Halberstam 1998: 77).

ONE MIGHT QUESTION WHETHER IT IS USEFUL TO STUDY female masculinity in popular culture. Should we not be more concerned with cutting edge gender theory and analysis, or even with real-life manifestations of gender transgressions? Inness explains:

> One reason it is crucial to study the representation of tough women is the tremendous influence popular culture has upon American society. With the postmodern blurring of boundaries between high and low culture, greater numbers of scholars have recognized the importance of studying popular culture in order to better comprehend our society. Popular sources are invaluable when exploring the changing image of women in our society. *Popular culture does not simply reflect women's lives; it helps to create them and so demands critical scrutiny.* (Inness 1999: 6-7, my emphasis)

Moreover, many of the filmic texts I analyze are part of the science fiction genre. If popular culture has a hard time being taken seriously, the problem is often compounded for science fiction, which may be perceived as fantasy that has limited relevance to real life. However, as has been pointed out by many renowned theorists, including Darko Suvin in *Metamorphoses of Science Fiction* and Ursula Le Guin, science fiction serves a unique purpose as a barometer of social change, for in its speculations about unknown futures it routinely engages with current problems, suggesting alternatives as yet unrealized. Thus, women's changing roles in society often appear first in science fiction. Moreover, "Not only does science fiction reflect women's roles, but it has the potential to re-envision and even alter gender roles" (Inness 1999: 104). Inness (1999) quotes critic Nadya Aisenberg, who has commented that science fiction offers a broad "opportunity to upset gender stereotypes and, beyond that, present visions of societies different from the one we inhabit" (Inness 1999: 104). Such a society is, for example, the one inhabited by Ripley in *Alien*, in which a woman can take over command of a space ship without so much as an eyebrow being raised by any of the crew. Similarly, no one was remotely surprised when Captain Kathryn Janeway authoritatively strode out onto the deck of the Starship *Voyager*, in the series by that name. (Janeway's role as the captain of *Voyager* is fully discussed in Chapter 4.)

Thus, I contend that science fiction, so far from being irrelevant, in fact constitutes a challenge to our current gender binary and the strict (and often ignominious) roles it imposes on women. Indeed, it may be seen as doing its part to stir up the kinds of transgressive gender trouble that Butler (1990) called for. Moreover, opening our society's hegemonic discourse to the possibility of alternative yet authentic gender expressions not only makes it possible for greater gender equity to be achieved, but also offers the exciting potential of making our world more inclusive of those on the sidelines, who often have difficulty finding their place in the tightly controlled world of the rigid gender binary system, and its concomitant, compulsory heterosexuality. For example,

Butler recalls that she was motivated to write her ground-breaking book, *Gender Trouble* (1990), because she wanted to "… counter those views that made presumptions about the limits and propriety of gender and restricted the meaning of gender to received notions of masculinity and femininity" (Butler 1990: vii). As Butler realized, this project should ultimately help the many people who do not fit neatly into the strictly defined gender binary. As Butler puts it, referring once again to *Gender Trouble*:

> … the aim of the text was to open up
> the field of possibility for gender without
> dictating which kinds of possibilities ought
> to be realized. One might wonder what use
> "opening up the possibilities" finally is, but
> no one who has understood what it is to live
> in the social world as what is "impossible,"
> illegible, unrealizable, unreal and illegitimate
> is likely to pose that question. (1990: vii)

A woman who has lived in the social world with a gender expression that is deemed "impossible" recalls her childhood search for viable role models:

> When I was little, I could recognize myself
> in the faces and screen characters of Tatum
> O'Neal, Jodie Foster, and Kristy McNichol.
> These little tomboys empowered me to think
> of myself as a hero. They were strong
> and smart like the movie cowboys and
> gangsters I emulated …. (Quoted in
> Halberstam 1998: 175)

Clearly, this "tomboy" girl found in screen "tomboys" role models that were compatible with her own reality, her own imagination, and her own preferred mode of gender expression. Unfortunately, as this child got older, the female role models she had found in films. She continues:

> As a young butch dyke coming out in 1986, I
> looked for their grown-up counterparts.
> I couldn't find anything. My trio of tomboy
> heroes hadn't turned out like I had. Instead,
> I turned to Marlon Brando and James Dean
> as my models of butchness.[9] (Quoted in
> Halberstam 1998: 175)

While this young woman could find no adult masculine female role models, in the two decades since 1986 such female role models have increasingly entered popular culture. Moreover, feminist theory such as that espoused by Halberstam and Butler has made explicit the falsity of biological essentialism. However, it still remains for these phenomena to be affirmed within the hegemonic discourse of our society. No less is required than that this discourse must affirm that female masculinity is as authentic as male masculinity, or female femininity, or male femininity – that, in short, gender expressions or performances may be as multifaceted as the weather, and none of them is less "real" or authentic than another. Indeed, as Butler has made clear, all gender positions are constructed: none is "natural" or "given" in any way.

In this book, I highlight the female masculinity expressed by female action heroes in popular, recent filmic texts. I use the term "recent" to denote texts published or released since 1979. This is directly related to the foundation of my argument, that is, the paradoxical fact that while female masculinity is becoming ever more visible in popular culture, its existence is nevertheless unacknowledged in the popular consciousness and in most academic discourses. Thus, the selection of popular texts is intended to substantiate Halberstam's assertion that female masculinity is, in fact, far more commonplace than is generally acknowledged. In the broader sense, this book attempts to contribute to the growing body of analysis of transgressive gender behaviors in literature, and more broadly, in popular culture. In a more specific sense, it aims to make more visible the reality of female masculinity in popular culture, in an attempt to contribute to the eventual validation of this mode of gender expression. The actor Tony Curtis has been quoted as follows:

> Movies are part of my life – part of everybody's life. That's where we learn about life. Watching Cary Grant taught me how to behave with a woman, how to get dressed at night, how to go to a restaurant and order dinner. (Quoted in Epstein and Freeman 1995)

MOVIES TAUGHT TONY CURTIS HOW TO BEHAVE *WITH* a woman, and they also taught many women how to behave *as* women. For far too long, movies taught that "cowering in corners" was the way for a woman to behave. This has changed, in that women have been depicted as a new envisioning of the traditional action hero, and in so doing have taken on many traditionally masculine behaviors.

This must be acknowledged and validated, so that more women are able to achieve greater freedom in real life. In this book I aim to make the representation of female masculinity embodied in the new female action hero more explicit. To do this, I will consider first the advent of female action heroes in the world of popular film, beginning with Ripley in the *Alien* series, which burst onto the screen in 1979. The *Alien* series and *Terminator 2* will be the primary focus of Chapter 3. Then, in Chapter 4, I will discuss female action heroes on the small screen. The primary focus will be the titular hero of the show *Buffy the Vampire Slayer*, although several other female action heroes will also be discussed, notably Xena, Warrior Princess and Captain Kathryn Janeway. Finally, in Chapter 5, I will draw together the implications of the advent and success of these female action heroes.

NOTES

1 Although there were some exceptions, as demonstrated by the fact that the word "queer," with its contemporary meaning, was in use before the middle of the twentieth century.

2 In this book, I mean "gender" in the sense of the behaviors associated with a biological sex, rather than merely the biological sex itself.

3 Note that this applies to Western society specifically. The context for this book is Western society. While it is acknowledged that this is exclusionary, it is regrettably beyond the scope of this book to attempt to be inclusive of all societies.

4 Those who do are a minority, often self-identified as transsexuals, and are beyond the scope of this book.

5 Nevertheless, it must be noted that most people at the time of the novel's publication in 1928 were in no doubt that this was a novel about lesbianism, and many were deeply offended. In fact, the novel became the subject of an obscenity trial in the UK later in 1928, with the magistrate ruling that the book was obscene in that it defended what he termed "unnatural practices between women." Thus, it fitted the definition of obscenity as something which tended to deprave and corrupt those whose minds are open to such immoral influences. The magistrate opined that no reasonable person could say that a plea for the recognition and toleration of inverts was not obscene. Consequently, all copies of the book were ordered destroyed.

6 In this book, the phrase "compulsory heterosexuality" refers to the theory that the rigid gender binary, in prescribing just two opposite sexes, also implies that the only authentic way of expressing sexuality is by a union of these two opposites. The poet Adrienne Rich introduced this phrase in her 1980 essay, "Compulsory Heterosexuality and Lesbian Existence". Rich linked compulsory heterosexuality to the politics of the patriarchal system. The concepts of the gender binary and compulsory heterosexuality are clearly natural bed-mates.

7 Alternatively, she might have opted to utilize medical technology to transition to male. Note that the term "transition" is used in keeping with current practice among the transgendered community in North America. The term "sex change" has been rejected by most, partly because this clearly implies *change*, whereas many in this community contend that they have *always been* the gender that they transition to. In this community, gender is seen as psychological, and the outward, physical manifestation frequently is seen as some kind of mistake, which can be corrected with hormones and surgery if one transitions to a more appropriate physical gender presentation. I am not in any way whatsoever seeking to imply that medically-aided gender transitioning is an inauthentic choice, as has been argued for example by Janice Raymond in *The Transsexual Empire: The Making of the She-Male* (1979). On the contrary, it is suggested that such transitioning should rather be seen as yet another authentic way of expressing gender.

8 Several feminist theorists, including Nancy Chodorow in *The Reproduction of Mothering* and Mary Poovey in *The Proper Lady and the Woman Writer,* have noted the equation between masculinity and public achievement.

9 In this book, "butchness" is regarded as one specific manifestation of female masculinity – a manifestation that is most commonly associated with masculine females who are also lesbian.

CHAPTER 3

FEMALE ACTION HEROES BURST ONTO THE SCREEN: RIPLEY AND OTHER HEROIC WOMEN IN RECENT FILMS

GIANT STRIDES WERE TAKEN IN FEMINIST AND GENDER identity theory during the latter half of the twentieth century, so that it became possible for many people to conceive of the gender of human beings as existing in a realm beyond the strict dictates of biological essentialism. Some gender theorists went so far as to conceptualize all gender as performance. However, despite such inroads, most action films have traditionally featured stereotypical male heroes such as those played by John Wayne, Clint Eastwood, Arnold Schwarzenegger, Sylvester Stallone, Bruce Willis, Jean-Claude van Damme and Will Smith – all of whom epitomize extreme masculinity, in undeniably male bodies. Recently, however, some action films have begun to feature female heroes – despite the fact that female heroes by definition are in violation of the gender binary and its assigned roles. As noted by Hills:

> ... one of the reasons why action heroines
> have been difficult to conceptualize as
> heroic female characters is the binaristic
> logic of the theoretical models on which a
> number of feminist theorists have relied.
> ... psychoanalytic accounts, which theorize
> sexual differences within the framework of
> linked binary opposition (active male/passive
> female), necessarily position normative
> female subjectivity as passive or in terms
> of lack. From this perspective, active and
> aggressive women in the cinema can only
> be seen as phallic, unnatural or "figuratively
> male." (Hills 1999: 38)

Clearly, viewed through a lens that explicitly rejects the binary dualism of gender and instead sees gender and gender traits as essentially free from the dictates of biology, it is in fact possible instead to view active and aggressive women in filmic texts as entirely natural, and entirely female.

THESE FEMALE CHARACTERS ARE BLAZING A TRAIL FOR ALL women, in the sense that they are claiming the right to be heroic – something that has for a long time been largely reserved for men. They are living out the dreams of the little girl in Alice Munro's story, "Girls and Boys":

> I arranged myself tightly under the covers
> and went on with one of the stories I was

telling myself from night to night. These stories were about myself, when I had grown a little older; they took place in a world that was recognizably mine, yet one that presented opportunities for courage, boldness and self-sacrifice, as mine never did. I rescued people from a bombed building …. I shot two rabid wolves who were menacing the schoolyard (the teachers cowered terrified at my back). I rode a fine horse spiritedly down the main street of Jubilee, acknowledging the townspeople's gratitude for some yet-to-be-worked-out piece of heroism …. There was always riding and shooting in these stories ….
(Munro 1996: 113-14)

By the end of this sad story, the little girl has given up her dreams, and has resigned herself to the tight confines that are prescribed for her by her society – a society that decrees that she may never be anything but "only a girl" (Munro 1996: 116). However, the female action heroes in many recent films have been freed from such constraints, and are able to live out dreams of heroism. Some do so while retaining the outward trappings associated with femininity and heterosexuality, while others cast these off to varying degrees. In so doing, they illustrate the far wider realm of gender expressions that are increasingly becoming available to women – and they illustrate graphically that women indeed can be masculine heroes; that being female-bodied does not preclude the traditionally masculine behaviors associated with traditional heroism.

IT IS USEFUL AT THIS POINT TO REPEAT MY DEFINITION OF female masculinity, to facilitate easy reference to the filmic texts and characters I examine in this chapter.

> **Female masculinity is a particular expression or performance of masculinity, an expression or performance that is entirely authentic, and that consists in female-bodied persons engaging in ways of thought and behaviour that have traditionally been considered masculine, such as claiming the right to authority, or displaying strength, courage, assertiveness, leadership, physicality (and sometimes violence), and very often heroism.**

Thus, female masculinity consists in female-bodied people expressing characteristics that have traditionally been considered quintessentially masculine. As is apparent from the above list of ways of thought or behavior, all of these masculine attributes are intrinsic parts of being heroic.

A review of popular films since 1979 reveals a broad range of films featuring heroic women. For the sake of analysis, it is useful to divide them into three groups. These groups are thematic rather than chronological. I will list them first, to provide a comprehensive overview, and then expand on the characteristics displayed by female heroes in each group.

❖ **GROUP 1:** Films in which conventionally beautiful, feminine, and usually heterosexual women assume many masculine prerogatives, such as power and strength. While these women display masculine behaviors, they also follow most of the rules that usually constrain the behavior of women – at least in terms of outward appearances. Examples of these films are *Buffy the Vampire Slayer* (1992) and *Barb Wire* (1996). Buffy epitomizes this group when she fearlessly and aggressively dispatches a band of vampires – and then laments that she has broken one of her beautifully-manicured nails. While this is played largely for laughs, it makes a crucial point.

❖ **GROUP 2:** These are films in which the women are much like those in Group 1, in terms of displaying masculine behaviors – but they break the mould by not *caring* whether they break a nail. Examples of these films are the *Alien* series and *Terminator 2*.

❖ **GROUP 3:** These are films in which women break all of the rules that usually constrain the behavior of women. They kick butt, and they simply do not care how they look. Like Ellen Ripley in the *Alien* series, they physically remove feminine markers such as long hair – but they take an extra step in that they *explicitly lay claim to male prerogatives*. While Ripley may be said to transcend gender categories, these women seem rather to cross over and join the men. Examples of such films are *The Long Kiss Goodnight* (1996) and *GI Jane* (1997).

I begin with **Group 1**: Films in which beautiful, feminine, heterosexual women assume many masculine prerogatives, such as power and strength. Tung (2004) refers to these women as the "new heroines," and says of them:

> ... these heroines all share in common
> portrayals as "kick-ass" women who can
> physically power their way out of dangerous
> situations using any combination of
> weaponry and martial arts, all the while
> maintaining traditional signs of femininity.
> (2004: 97)

Yet while these women look like sex objects, they are anything but – as was made clear by the poster advertising the film *Barb Wire*, which showed a leather-clad Barb Wire, crouching to aim a large gun, besides the giant, bold words "DON'T CALL ME BABE!"

Group 1 includes films like *Buffy the Vampire Slayer* (1992); *Barb Wire* (1996); *Tomb Raider* (2001); *Crouching Tiger Hidden Dragon* (2003); *Kill Bill I* (2003) and *Kill Bill II* (2004); as well as television series such as *Buffy the Vampire Slayer* (1997 to 2003); *Xena, Warrior Princess* (1995 to 2001); and *La Femme Nikita* (1997 to 2001) (television series will be further discussed in Chapter 4).

Perhaps the most interesting thing about the female heroes in this group of films is that they combine traits that have for long been considered entirely antithetical, if not oxymoronic. For example, the Buffy character played by Kirsty Swanson in the 1992 film version of *Buffy the Vampire Slayer* takes on all of the most important attributes of the traditional male hero: she accepts her responsibility to protect the world from vampires, she kills vampires with relish, she protects her boyfriend (Pike, played by Luke Perry), and in general saves the world. As writer/creator Joss Whedon says: "The very first mission statement of the show, was the joy of female power: having it, using it, sharing it" (Gottlieb 2002).

But interestingly, when Buffy experiences hero-fatigue and doubts about her own capabilities, Pike encourages her with these words: "But Buffy, you're the guy. You *are* the chosen guy." The choice of wording here is very interesting, as Pike is in effect saying "You're the man" – using a terminology that is intensely masculine. Yet when Buffy dances with Pike at the end of the film, the following dialogue ensues:

PIKE: You're not like other girls, Buffy.
(Short silence.)
BUFFY: *(Slow and serious)* Yes ... I am.

And then, in the best tradition of the romance movie, they kiss ... Thus, Buffy's heterosexuality is re-established, minutes after she has finished routing the vampires. Pike is still the boy who got the girl, and Buffy is still the girl – who just happens to be a brave, undeniably masculine-acting superhero. Interestingly, the two have just agreed that *neither* of them will lead on the dance floor, indicating that the characters are conscious of needing to forge new gender norms to match their reality. This is true even though the dance floor may be seen as a traditionally "feminine" sphere, while the killing of monsters such as vampires is a traditionally "masculine" sphere.

THE WOMEN IN **GROUP 2** BEHAVE SIMILARLY TO THOSE IN Group 1. However, they break the mould by not caring about maintaining a traditionally feminine appearance. While the Buffy character in both the film and the television series versions garnered a lot of laughs by frequently checking her beautifully manicured nails after dispatching demons, the women in this group of films do not give a second thought to maintaining feminine appearances. As a result, they may be seen as moving a step further out of the rigid constraints of the gender binary, which have traditionally prescribed that women's value resides primarily in their feminine attractiveness (as it is this that makes them valuable to those who *really* matter – men). Thus, in order to be a "real woman," it was necessary to dress in a decorative way, emphasizing feminine attractiveness and signalling receptivity to men. The women in this group usually ignore this requirement of the gender binary. However, they remain for the most part heterosexual, or sometimes asexual – as for example Ripley, played by Sigourney Weaver in the *Alien* series, appears to be (except for a notable exception in the third film).[1] This is a smaller group of films, likely because it breaks the gender rules more, and it is epitomized by the two ground-breaking film series, *Alien* and *Terminator*. Ripley is widely acknowledged to be the first filmic female action hero. Inness (2004: 3) comments about her:

> Ripley demonstrated that women did not have to look as though they stepped directly from a beauty parlor when they battled foes. Following her lead, Linda Hamilton, as Sarah Connor starred in *The Terminator* (1984) and *Terminator 2: Judgment Day* (1991). A buff figure in the second film, she showed that women could compete with men as action-adventure heroes.

In the first *Alien* film, Ripley does not yet have the shaved head that later became so notorious. Instead, her hair is long and wavy, so that even in a military-style jumpsuit, Ripley is borderline feminine-looking. For the second *Alien* film, *Aliens* (1986), her hair has been cut back to shoulder-length, although she still has a perm.

HERE IT IS IMPORTANT TO NOTE THAT LONG HAIR is considered an important marker of female heterosexual attractiveness in the gender binary system. This system is predicated upon the assumption that heterosexual desire is fuelled by difference – the "bodily differences at the centre of heterosexual desire" (Ussher 57). Women's impractically long, often permed hair stands in stark contrast to the practical, no-nonsense short-back-and-sides (or even brush cut) sported by many macho men, and by action heroes such as John Wayne, Clint Eastwood, Arnold Schwarzenegger, Sylvester Stallone, Bruce Willis, Jean-Claude van Damme and Will Smith.

Heterosexual desire is assumed to be built largely on such bodily differences, so that when a woman wears her hair long and/or permed, she is assumed to be signifying that she is heterosexually available. Ussher (1997) records the experiences of lesbians who choose to wear long hair and who are then assumed to be part of the heterosexual system: "It's much easier if you cut off your hair and act butch. It feels more powerful. With long hair I was always being asked when I went out if I knew this was a gay club" (58).

On the other hand, women who for other reasons are at odds with the gender binary system may wear their hair long in a desperate attempt to fit into the system. For example, bodybuilding is a sport that is entirely at odds with the gender binary that holds that men are naturally strong, while women are naturally weak, for most women bodybuilders are stronger and more muscular than most men. As a result, "many people continue to see women bodybuilders as rebels or 'deviants,' as freaks of nature" (Coakley and Donnelly 2004: 243). In an attempt to be perceived as "normal" within the gender binary system, most competitive women bodybuilders attempt to feminize themselves as much as possible. Despite the fact that their bodies are lean, muscular and often breast-less, they will compete with long hair and heavy makeup. These women are well aware that their musculature is at odds with the gender binary-based stereotype of weak femininity, and therefore know they are in danger of social rejection (for example, being rejected as freaks or lesbians) if they do not strenuously strive to appear as much like the stereotype as is possible for someone whose biceps are the same size as the average man's thighs. Long hair is an essential part of this attempt, demonstrating the importance of long hair within the system of heterosexual objectification (Coakley and Donnelly 2004).

In strong contrast to the traditional feminine ideal of long hair, in the third *Alien* film (*Alien 3*, 1992) Ripley memorably sports no hair at all, after shaving it off to avoid getting lice in the male prison she has landed in. While Ripley thus pays decreasing attention to her "feminine" appearance, this is offset by the fact that she is, arguably, one of the most beautiful women in the world. For example, in the first *Alien* film, despite her (presumably simulated) absence of makeup, Ripley fills out her jumpsuit quite differently from the men, and with a dash of style, so that there can be no doubt she is indeed female-bodied.

HERE IT IS NECESSARY TO ACKNOWLEDGE THAT WOMEN action heroes confront a danger much more real than any fictional monster, and one, which is not faced by their male counterparts: they risk being entirely undermined merely by virtue of the fact that they are conventionally beautiful. For example, Laura Mulvey argues famously that the relations between the look of the camera, the look of the spectator and the looks of characters operate in such as way as to place the (male) spectator in a position of voyeuristic dominance over women, who comprise the primary sexualized object of the cinematic gaze. Thus, regardless of the fact that Ripley saves the world by killing monsters, Mulvey would contend that she is in fact subordinated because cinema by definition reduces her merely to her quality of "to-be-looked-atness" (relative to the male-centered look of the camera, and of the spectator). Mulvey refers to the male scopophilic gaze, and defines the scopophilic instinct as "pleasure in looking at another person as an erotic object" (1975: 18). She would no doubt see the famous (or infamous) scene in which Ripley strips down to her underwear[2] as fitting neatly into what she refers to as "that voyeuristic-scopophilic look that is a crucial part of traditional filmic pleasure" (Mulvey 1975: 18).

Certainly, one could make a strong argument for Mulvey's view, even for a female hero in what I have designated Group 2. After all, Weaver is a conventionally beautiful woman, and it is a very safe presumption that less conventionally beautiful women such as Kathy Bates were never in contention for the role. Thus, it could be argued that Ripley still panders to film audiences' expectations regarding feminine beauty on screen, and even that this negates her heroic status. However, I would argue that merely looking good in conventional terms does not undermine Ripley's heroic status, especially given the fact that she never adorns herself in any of the ways that have been traditionally prescribed for women to decorate themselves for the male eye. Moreover, both before and since Mulvey wrote about "that voyeuristic-scopophilic gaze" in 1975, there have been a succession of good-looking men who have played heroes, and no one suggests that their good looks undermine their heroic status. This is despite that fact that, for example, the camera's gaze (and therefore inevitably the spectators' eyes) lingers very lovingly indeed on Arnold Schwarzenegger's naked body, when he bursts in a bubble from the past to arrive in the present, at the beginning of *Terminator*. Similarly, at the beginning of *Terminator 2*, much is made of Schwarzenegger's nudity as he strolls into a bar in search of clothes, and is eyed with naked lust by more than one of the bar patrons. To add to his object status, the bar is hosting a male strip show, and he is mistaken for one of the performers. However, I have yet to read a review that lamented that Schwarzenegger had been stripped down to the status of mere sex object in *T2*. Similarly, the quintessential male action hero, Clint Eastwood, is remarkable for his good looks, especially in the films made in his youth, while Bruce Willis, Sylvester Stallone, Jean-Claude van Damme and Will Smith are scarcely painful to look at.

Clearly, women are viewed and presented differently from men in movies. However, my point is that if men can look good and still be taken seriously, women should be allowed the same leeway. I argue that Ripley's heroic status in *Alien* is such that she emerges clearly as a hero, irrespective of her good looks. Anyone at all who bravely confronted the horrific alien depicted in this film would be a hero, regardless of their physical appearance. The mere fact that the character who does this in this film is both a woman and conventionally beautiful does not change this, any more than it changes his heroic status when a male action hero happens to be conventionally good-looking (which is most often the case, Marlon Brando notwithstanding).

Indeed, I would go so far as to argue that Weaver's good looks add to the impact of her heroism in the first *Alien*, inasmuch as she is able to catch the audience off guard. After all, there had never before been a strong female action hero in any major Hollywood production, and the unsuspecting 1979 viewer would almost certainly have assumed that Ripley was merely there to look good and be a love interest for any or all of the male astronauts. (I saw this film when I was nineteen years old, and as a young connoisseur of both the science fiction and action movie genres, that was certainly my informed expectation. Happily, my expectation was crushed.) However, that misapprehension is rapidly corrected. Near the beginning of the film, the cargo space vessel *Nostromo* has landed on an unknown planet, in response to what appears to be a distress signal. Captain Dallas, Executive Officer Kane and Navigator Lambert (the only other woman, and also the pilot) have gone off to investigate. While away, an alien creature resembling a particularly repulsive, bony octopus attaches itself to Kane's face. The distressed trio returns to the spaceship, and desperately demands admittance. In the absence of both Dallas and Kane, Warrant Officer Ripley is the most senior officer aboard the ship. The following dialogue ensues:

DALLAS: Ripley, let us in!
RIPLEY: *(Warily)* What happened to Kane?
DALLAS: Something has attached itself to him – we have to get him to the Infirmary right away.
RIPLEY: *(Perturbed)* What kind of thing? I need a clear definition.

DALLAS: An organism. *(Becoming agitated)* Open the hatch!

RIPLEY: Wait a minute. If we let it in, the ship could be infected. You know the quarantine procedure – twenty-four hours for decontamination.

DALLAS: *(More agitated)* He could die in twenty-four hours – open the hatch!

RIPLEY: *(Quietly insistent)* Listen to me – if we break quarantine we could all die.

LAMBERT: *(Frantically)* Could you open the goddam hatch – we have to get him inside.

RIPLEY: *(Firmly)* No. I can't do that, and if you were in my position, you'd do the same.

DALLAS: *(Becoming angry)* Ripley, this is an order, open that hatch right now. Do you hear me?

RIPLEY: Yes.

DALLAS: *(Becoming hysterical)* Ripley, this is an order, do you hear me?

RIPLEY: *(Calm, resolute)* Yes, I read you, the answer is negative.

This brief interchange dramatically signals an extremely significant moment in movie history – the arrival of the first female action hero. From this moment, the audience knows that the true leader, and the only one who deserves to be commanding this ship, is Ripley. As noted by Hills (1999: 40):

> Ripley is, of course, a highly transgressive,
> transformative and controversial character.
> As, arguably, the first "action heroine" of
> her type, she entered our cultural imaginary
> almost twenty years ago and continues to
> be a significant cultural icon. Whilst there
> have been many examples of active women

in action genres (ranging from Emma Peel of *The Avengers* to the fashionable heroines of *Charlie's Angels*) the action heroine as I analyze her here emerged with Ripley from the *Alien* series. *Alien* is what Thomas Schatz calls a "new Hollywood blockbuster": a complete package with elaborate special effects, thirty-million dollar budget, expensive pre-release publicity and, most importantly, huge box-office success. It generated a series of (so far) three sequels, and Ripley has become one of Hollywood's most visible action heroines.

M OREOVER, THE AUDIENCE LEARNS THAT RIPLEY IS TO BE the hero in a context that subverts the traditional gender binary. Dallas is being "feminine" in letting his feelings about the needs of his fallen comrade get ahead of proper protocol and safety. In addition, he becomes hysterical[3] – behavior which was previously almost exclusive to female film characters, and which was certainly never in evidence from male captains of space ships. By contrast, Ripley remains calm and focused. Ripley is being "masculine" in the sense commonly seen in male action heroes. As Inness (1999: 106) puts it:

> Ripley is tough because she is willing to sacrifice her personal wish to save her fellow crew member for the greater good of the ship and its crew .... Here, we notice one common characteristic of the tough women in space. Ripley adheres to a higher code of

> morality than her fellows, and she is able to
> make the tough decisions no one else will.

Here, Ripley claims the authority to make the choice to save the four crew members on board, as well as the ship and its cargo. It is important to note that in so doing, Ripley steps beyond the confines of the concerns that have traditionally been assumed to be biologically prescribed for women, that is, the well-being of the domestic unit, as opposed to the well-being of society in general. A quintessential heroic quality is acting on behalf of other people, not just oneself or one's family. In the traditional view of the gender binary, women are effectively precluded from heroism because they are assumed to be biologically programmed to take care of and protect their families, with the concomitant flaw of having minds so limited by domesticity that they are unable to act for the sake of the "big picture." This quality of women may be ascribed to social conditioning that trains women to place the preservation of their families above all else. Alternatively, in extreme views such as biological determinism, it may be seen as genetic programming – the "maternal instinct" which supersedes all other imperatives. Here, however, Ripley makes the "tough decision" to put the needs of the many ahead of the needs of the few, and in so doing assumes a quintessential heroic quality. She continues to do this throughout the duration of the series of *Alien* films.

In assuming the responsibility for the ship, unlike countless female film characters before her, Ripley does not for a second bow to male authority, or question her own wisdom when it is challenged by someone who is not only a man, but also her commanding officer. If the crew had listened to Ripley, she would have saved the day and they would all have been spared grisly deaths (apart from Kane, who was already doomed, and Ripley, who eventually is the sole survivor). However, Science Officer Ash (who later turns out to be a robot programmed to bring the alien creature back to earth, regardless of consequences) breaks protocol by ignoring Ripley's orders, and lets the threesome in – and the nightmare begins. As the film progresses, the audience is introduced to arguably the most frightening creature that has ever scarred the silver screen – a creature that gave rise to the cultural catch phrase (used on the posters advertising the movie), "In space, no one can hear you scream." And while Ripley is heard to scream once or twice, she is unfailingly courageous, and eventually defeats the monster with a combination of grit, intelligence and a perfectly aimed shot. No male hero had ever done a better job – and the female action hero was well and truly launched.

R IPLEY NOT ONLY LAUNCHED THE FEMALE ACTION HERO, but also epitomized what I have termed Group 2 female action heroes: she is conventionally beautiful, but pays not so much as lip service to the societal dictates that women should focus their intelligence and energy on making themselves heterosexually attractive. The women in the group I define as **Group 3** take this a step further. Like Ripley in *Alien*, they physically remove feminine markers such as long hair – but they also take an extra step, in that they explicitly lay claim to male prerogatives. While Ripley may be said to transcend (or perhaps merely ignore) gender categories, these women seem rather to cross over and join the men. This group is epitomized by films such as *GI Jane* (1997) and *The Long Kiss Goodnight* (1996). In *GI Jane*, Lieutenant Jordan

O'Neil (played memorably by Demi Moore) attempts to invade the all-male preserve of the US Marines. She puts her femininity behind her, symbolically, when she shaves off all of her long hair to become "one of the boys." She then participates in a training experience reminiscent of the film *Rocky*, culminating in a scene in which she out-machos the most macho of men by performing pushups with one arm. By this time, her periods have stopped, and her body is looking noticeably hard and muscular. Thus, she is literally becoming more androgynous, and her appearance is beginning to conform more to the masculine ideal than the feminine. Most notably, she emulates Charly in the previous year's *The Long Kiss Goodnight* when she tells the master chief to "Suck my dick!"

This memorable scene occurs during one of O'Neil's many clashes with Master Chief John James Urgayle. O'Neil's squad has just been taken hostage in a simulation, and O'Neil has engaged in bloody hand-to-hand combat with Urgayle. While some of the spectators are shocked that Urgayle is hurting a woman, O'Neil takes it "like a man." She survives the punches, and manages to kick the Master Chief, even though her arms are handcuffed behind her back. As she does so, she screams, "Suck my dick!" eliciting the admiration of her male comrades, who then join her in a group chant of "Suck my dick!" The solidarity of the squad and its toughness under pressure is demonstrated in this group expression of contempt for the "enemy." Moreover, O'Neil herself is transformed by this moment:

> In their essay about the gun as metaphorical masculinization in *GI Jane*, Tucker and Fried rightly observe that it is at this moment,

> as she "basks in the cheers and acceptance
> of her fellow recruits, [that] O'Neil's
> transformation into a rugged, individualistic
> techno-male is complete." (Brown 2004: 56).

This scene (unsurprisingly) has elicited mixed reactions. Notably, an explicitly queer commentator states that it is a moment when gender roles are challenged as O'Neil lets "her butch side shine. It's a moment when a woman taking on the male gender role is celebrated and it's not only cinematically exciting but also profoundly moving" (Nova 2007).

Similarly, while Samantha/Charly in *The Long Kiss Goodnight* never looks anything but attractive, she adopts an extremely macho screen presence as Charly, and in the climatic moments of the action portion of the film, shouts "Suck my dick, every last one of you bastards!" as she drives a huge truck straight towards her enemies, unconcerned by the explosions all around her. Her feminine attractiveness recedes into the background in the face of this explicit, transgressive appropriation of male power. Williams notes that the most cursory knowledge of psychoanalysis informs us that "dick" equates to power – that power to which most people aspire, regardless of anatomy. In the same vein, Brown (2004) argues that when Charly and O'Neil lay claim to the traits of maleness, they:

> … gain access to a form of power
> (both physical and social) that has been
> systematically denied to women while
> simultaneously demonstrating that the
> association of "maleness" with "power"

is not innate but culturally defined since
anyone can mobilize even the most basic of
male privileges: the privilege to assert phallic
authority through reference to an actual
phallus. (57)

In the discussion above, I differentiate groups of female
action heroes with reference to physical presentation –
the degree to which the heroes attempt to conform to the
traditional social requirement associated with the gender
binary, that is, the requirement for women to present
themselves as decorative and "feminine," so that men will find
them attractive. However, it is notable that this discussion led
to the point where, in Group 3, some women who eschew
such requirements simultaneously lay claim to male traits,
and hence might be perceived as crossing over the gender
divide. This brings me to a key point argued by many critics
– the contention that female heroes are not transgressive or
liberatory at all, but are merely men in drag. For example,
Inness (1999) argues that:

Ripley is forced into femininity's opposite,
masculinity, which makes her like a man. In
our culture femininity and masculinity are
in opposition and therefore exclude one
another. Thus toughness for Ripley is not
some new feminist ideal, where she takes the
best parts of femininity and masculinity and
forges them into a type of toughness that
has not yet been seen. Instead, Ripley can
be perceived as a man in a woman's body,
reason enough for critics to complain about

her being just another Rambo figure.
(Inness 1999: 107)

However, I argue that in making this point, Inness (1999) is unduly constrained by the gender binary, specifically the psychoanalytical model which Hills (1999) identifies as positioning "female characters as the passive, immobile and peripheral characters of Hollywood action cinema" (Hills 1999: 38), and men as their exact opposite.

T HE POINT IS THAT RIPLEY TRANSCENDS THIS ARTIFICIAL, socially-constructed divide, thus transgressing cultural gender codes and opening up "interesting questions about the fluidity of gendered identities" (Hills 1999: 38). Hence, Ripley is not "forced into femininity's opposite." On the contrary, she voluntarily embraces a gender expression that is – or potentially could be – available to all women, a gender expression that includes traditionally masculine behaviors such as aggression towards enemies, concern for the greater good, claiming the right to authority, decisive leadership, assertiveness and courage, but which at the same time does not deprive Ripley of the ability to express feminine behaviors, such as caring for cats or children.

In order to argue her point, Inness (1999) ignores the hour in which Ripley battles monsters with steely courage, and instead focuses on the penultimate scene of *Alien*, in which Ripley appears clad in very scanty underwear. She perceives this as emphasizing the fact that Ripley "is a girl" (Inness 1999: 107), and concludes that ultimately the "film seems uncomfortable leaving viewers with an image of Ripley that is too tough" (Inness 1999: 107). However, what Inness (1999) (as well as many other critics who have singled out this particular scene as evidence of Ripley being transformed into an object, or transformed back into femininity) glosses over is what happens *next*. Ripley realizes that the alien is still very much alive and on board the space ship and immediately dons appropriate apparel to wage a final battle with the alien. In this battle she unequivocally defeats the alien, and finally ejects it into space. Like so many creatures that have dared to take on male heroes, this beast dies screaming – but this time, it is a woman who administers the death blows, and saves the earth from a devastating invasion (as the creature's ultimate destination was earth).

I argue (at the risk of butchering Inness) that in these two final scenes, Ripley's toughness is indeed "some new feminist ideal," in which she takes the best parts of femininity and masculinity and forges them into a type of toughness that has not yet been seen. In doing so, she transgressively draws together the realms of femininity and masculinity. Yes, she is both vulnerable and alluring in her underwear. Thus, for a few brief (albeit memorable) moments, she enters the traditional realm of femininity. However, when circumstances change (that is, when she realizes the alien enemy is still on board), she is able to shift gears, effortlessly assuming – both literally and metaphorically – the apparel of the hero, and calmly dispatching the monster. Ripley thus adapts flexibly to changing circumstances, deploying appropriate behaviors to deal with them. In this, she epitomizes Deleuze's notion of "becoming" (Deleuze and Guattari 1987: 232–309). In Deleuzian terms, one might say that Ripley's actions exceed our concepts of feminine passivity by presenting the novelty of Ripley exhibiting behaviors traditionally associated with masculinity and with men, and this novel representation then actualizes an idea which is unfettered by prior categories based on an acceptance of the gender binary. Ripley's gender expression is more transgressive than if she were merely "acting like a man." Instead, she is acting like, or performing as (and at the same time becoming) something entirely new: a female-bodied person who freely chooses from a range of hitherto gender-linked behaviors to create a new mix that enables her to be a new kind of hero. She becomes a specifically female hero, not just a woman behaving like the archetypal male hero. It should also be noted here that Ripley epitomizes Judith Butler's notion of gender roles as performativity, for she can switch from performing femininity so well that hosts of critics have been blinded by it (as in the penultimate scene where she strips to her underwear), to performing masculinity so well that she is able to save the world (as in the final scene where she kills the alien queen).

THIS BLENDING OF GENDER ROLES IS OF COURSE NOT AN easy mix to accomplish. It is not only Inness (1999) who is constrained by the stark opposites of the gender binary. They are deeply embedded in our culture, and hence in all of us. In this regard, *The Long Kiss Goodnight* is an interesting film, as its central focus appears to be the conflicts inherent in transgressing the gender divide and daring to attempt to embrace behaviors from both sides within one human being. The hero, Samantha *aka* Charly (played winningly by the conventionally lovely Geena Davis), epitomizes a key conflict. As noted previously, hitherto "action heroines have been difficult to conceptualize as heroic female characters ... [because of] the binaristic logic of ... theoretical models" (Hills 1999: 39). As Hills (1999) points out, even many feminist theorists have been unable to conceive of female heroes because of the constraints of such models. Samantha/Charly epitomizes the conflicts engendered by this strict binaristic logic. The first hint is of course that she has two names, one of which is masculine, and the other feminine. She does not know which is her "real" name, as she has amnesia. Throughout the film, she wrestles with the conflict between her masculine side and her feminine side, like a latter-day Jekyll and Hyde. The possibility of reconciling the two does not come to the fore until the very end of the film. Indeed, Brown (2004) has gone so far as to argue that in *The Long Kiss Goodnight*, the "real plot is the gender negotiation of feminine Samantha into masculine Charly and then the final attempt at a reconciliation between the two persons at film's end" (55).

Clearly, a successful reconciliation could be liberatory, but the liberatory potential of the film has been dismissed by some critics. For example, Brown (2004) states that the "self-discovery of *The Long Kiss Goodnight* is a literal stripping away of the feminine masquerade embodied by Samantha in favor of the underling masculine character of Charly" (54). However, Brown (2004) fails to notice that when Charly goes into action to rescue her young daughter, Cataline, she effectively draws together the two parts of her personality that Brown sees as mutually exclusive – the feminine and the masculine. Femininity is routinely linked to the maternal imperative, and when the more masculine Charly first emerges from the more feminine Samantha (as the latter regains her memory of her former persona), her first reaction is to walk away from her maternal responsibilities. In this, she shows herself to be a victim of binaristic gender thinking. However, later in the film she is able to reconcile the masculine and the feminine, using the masculine traits associated with an action hero to rescue her daughter and dispatch the bad guys. Thus,

Charly/Samantha takes the action hero to a new and I would say a better level: a level where the action hero can embody the best of both feminine and masculine traits. This film therefore underscores the point that although it is difficult for one person to perform actions that are conventionally attributed to both sexes, it is not impossible – and that the new female action hero succeeds admirably in doing precisely this.

I T IS CLEAR THAT THE ESSENCE OF THE TRANSFORMATIVE POWER OF the female action hero is that she makes possible a new way of *behaving*, rather than a new way of *appearing*. Thus, while my exposition of the three groups above emphasizes physical appearance, my key points about female action heroes pertain to far more than the merely physical. While this aspect attracts much attention, the most important point is that many female action heroes exhibit behaviors that transcend the traditional binary gender divide, thus making possible a far richer and more interesting heroic archetype.

However, I argue that what we may take from the wide range of physical manifestations of female action heroes is that it is possible for a women to be a female action hero, regardless of how she happens to look. This is a liberatory way of looking at it. The message it sends to young female viewers is clear: you can look like Barbie, and still kick butt like Rambo. You can have beautiful nails, but still be a fearless leader, or save the world. On the other hand, if you explicitly don't *want* to look like Barbie, that too is your prerogative. Moreover, given the clear examples set by cool-headed, intelligent leaders such as Ripley, the other lesson is that women no longer merely have the right to change their minds – they have the right to *have* minds. This of course challenges conventional assumptions, which equate men with the cognitive, and deny rationality to women.

In short, the truly exciting thing about female action heroes is that some of them have broadened the understanding of what it is to be a hero, and in so doing have revisioned not only women, but also the traditional hero archetype. They have done this by incorporating a range of traditionally female behaviors into the representation of a hero, such as the maternal instinct, flexibility, sharing and a talent for and enjoyment of communication.

ANOTHER EXAMPLE OF A FEMALE HERO REVISIONING THE heroic archetype by incorporating the maternal instinct may be found in the very first female hero, Ripley. In the first film, *Alien*, Ripley invests more than a little energy in saving her cat. In the second film, *Aliens*, this is taken a step further, when Ripley rescues a little girl, Newt, and later risks her own life to save her from the alien queen. It is also notable here that little Newt is a hero in her own right, having exhibited the toughness to survive while all of the other colonists, including her parents and her brother, have been killed by aliens. This is a point routinely ignored in commentaries on the film, most of which perceive Newt merely as a victim to be saved. Moreover, as pointed out by Inness (1999), some critics have taken Ripley's concern for Newt to undermine her status as a hero. However, such critics missed the point that Ripley was a hero long before she met Newt, and remains a hero long after Newt dies. Thus, she is not a stereotypical woman motivated only by maternal concerns. Indeed, her primary concern is always to save the earth – like all of the hyper-rational, heroic captains of star ships in the *Star Trek* series, Ripley remains always focused on the greater good. However, I argue that she broadens the concept of the action hero by being able to incorporate within it her maternal concern for young Newt. Moreover, in her interactions with Newt, Ripley is able to show a wider range of emotions than have traditionally been available to (male) action heroes. For example, Newt says, "Ripley, I'm scared" – and Ripley replies, simply, "Me too." Thus, Ripley has the normal emotions that anyone would have while trapped in a building surrounded by thousands of hostile, powerful monsters – notably fear. Unlike many action heroes before her, she is able to both feel fear and admit to it. However, unlike the screaming, cowering women of science fiction films before her – such as Anne Francis as Altaira Morbius in *Forbidden Planet* (Wilcox 1956), who screams helplessly as the monster created by her father's sub conscious threatens her loved ones – she is not incapacitated by her fear. Instead, she remains capable of fighting for her life and the lives of her companions, especially Newt.

As in the first *Alien* film, Ripley fights to save others. However, this is a different, more mature Ripley. She has evolved to become a more confident hero. For example, the first time she is given orders by the inexperienced, out-of-his-depth Commanding Officer Gorman, she simply ignores him – she is going in to save the embattled marines from the alien's nest, regardless of his orders. Thus, she has progressed from the emotional immaturity she showed at the beginning of the first *Alien* film, when she was merely a company woman taking orders. She no longer trusts the company (which is synonymous with power, and thus may be read as symbolic of the patriarchy), nor does she take orders unless they make sense for the preservation of life in the battle against the aliens. However, she continues to learn from others, such as Corporal Hicks, when he teaches her how to handle a large gun (one of many obvious phallic symbols adroitly handled by Ripley in this film). However, there is no male patronizing going on here. She tells him coolly: "I can handle myself" and he readily agrees: "Yeah, I noticed." She also learns from Newt, who directs them through the heating ducts to the landing field. Thus, we have the transgressive situation of a little girl leading soldiers to safety – again underlining the heroic status of this small girl.

Later, in the third *Alien* film, *Alien 3*, Ripley is the only woman on the planet, and yet it is to her that the embattled prisoners turn for leadership when their lives are threatened by aliens. This film has been much criticized, with allegations that Ripley compromises her heroic status by being sexualized as the only woman in the prison, and also by killing herself at the end, so that "her death serves as a warning to women who, like Ripley, might rebel against gender constraints and adopt tough personas" (Inness 1999: 113).

However, I would argue that these allegations are misguided. On the contrary, Ripley shows her courage by managing to emerge as a leader in such threatening circumstances. In the previous *Alien* films, she only had to fear the aliens. In this film, she is in danger from the humans as well. However, she continues undaunted, displaying her heroic status in these extremely challenging circumstances. In this I suggest that she transcends the heroic levels of male heroes, in that male action heroes never have to carry out their heroic missions while at the same time worrying about being raped by a prison-full of criminals. Moreover, her death at the end of the movie is a heroic self-sacrifice, not a lesson to other women to kowtow to gender norms. Throughout the first three *Alien* films, Ripley is unswervingly committed to the greater good, in the best heroic tradition – and in her final act in the third film, she takes this commitment to its ultimate expression. In addition, by doing this, she endeavours to keep out of the (male) hands of the Company a potential weapon that would undoubtedly be used to devastating effect (that is, the alien that is incubating inside her). She falls backward into a vat of boiling lead, and as she does so, the incubating alien bursts out of her. She uses her last ounce of dying strength to hold onto the alien and make sure that it dies with her, so the company cannot get it. As she says: "I don't think so." In the event, this alien is eventually revived by cloning, in the fourth film. However, this is hundreds of years in the future, so that Ripley's efforts are not entirely in vain – although it must be conceded that the film industry's commercially-motivated action in cloning Ripley for a fourth film do detract somewhat from Ripley's self-sacrifice at the end of the third film.

L IKE RIPLEY, THE CHARACTER OF SARAH CONNOR (played by Linda Hamilton) in the *Terminator* films also maintains an interesting balance of traditionally feminine qualities with traditionally male qualities. Most notable, of course, is that she has a dual motivation: to save the world and to protect her son (who is destined to save the world). She thus combines the public and domestic within the ambit of one person, and takes responsibility for what are viewed as the traditionally male heroic spheres, as well as the traditionally female domestic ones. However, when the first *Terminator* film begins, Sarah Connor is a stereotypically feminine woman, dewy-eyed, conventionally lovely, and curvaceous. She works as a waitress (ineptly) and shares an apartment with another young woman. One day, a terminator (played by Arnold Schwarzenegger), a cyborg,[4] arrives from the future to kill her, and thus ensure the victory of machines over humans in the future war (by ensuring her son is never born, and thus cannot lead the surviving humans to victory). Sarah's life descends into immediate chaos, as she flees for her life pursued by a relentless and immensely powerful killing machine. Just then, another being arrives from the future — a human named Kyle Reece, who has been sent by Sarah's future son, John Connor, to protect her. Initially, the relationship between the two of them is stereotypical. As in *Alien*, the audience is lulled into expected that the male hero will save the passive female victim — especially when she looks at Reece with big dewy eyes and asks pathetically, "Can you stop him?"

The first time Sarah Connor assumes control is when she realizes that Reece has been injured, and insists on treating his wound. Thus, she takes her first step towards power in the traditionally female roles of healer and caretaker. Reece then tells her that he volunteered to come through time to meet her because she is a legend, the one who trained the future champion of humanity, John Connor — but Sarah finds this hard to believe. The first time she is handed a gun, she puts it down in disgust — but then almost immediately picks it up again. This classic phallic symbol, used to connote aggressive masculinity in countless films, is the almost immediate object of her curiosity. This is the first clue that Sarah may morph from bimbo to hero. Very soon she is learning to make bombs, under the tutelage of Reece. She then takes on the traditionally masculine role when she initiates sex with him (the act which will lead to the birth of her son John, who is destined to save the world). As with Ripley before her, the only time Sarah is depicted having sex is when she herself initiates the act. Moreover, when they have sex, she is on top – again appropriating the traditionally masculine role. If that does not suffice to make it clear that the gender-binary table has been turned, the very next morning she saves Reece from certain death, by dragging him out of the way of a speeding juggernaut driven by the Terminator.

Shortly thereafter, both Sarah and Reece think that the Terminator is dead – but then he rises again. Sarah screams just once, before she begins to drag the injured Kyle away, and shouts at him: "On your feet, soldier, on your feet!" Clearly, Sarah is becoming a hero, is adapting to circumstances, and is embracing within herself both feminine and masculine attributes in order to deal with her radically altered circumstances.

SARAH IS IN FACT "BECOMING," IN THE SENSE PROPOSED BY Deleuze: in Sarah, two systems (masculine and feminine) are coming together to form an emergent system – in this case, the new female action hero. Moreover, as with Ripley, we may relate Sarah's adaptability to Butler's work, noting that Sarah performs femininity when this suffices for the needs of her life, but is able to quickly adapt and perform masculinity when extreme circumstances demand it. This culminates in the penultimate scene of the film, when she leads the Terminator into a trap, and triumphantly tells him: "You're terminated, fucker." In the next and final scene, she is driving through the Mexican desert in an orange Renegade jeep, with a large German Shepherd in the back of the jeep, dictating memoirs to her unborn son. Her hair has less curl, and she sports a no-nonsense headband. When she stops to put gas in her jeep, a local tells her: "There's a storm coming in." Looking resolute, she agrees: "I know" – and then drives off towards the mountains. Of course, the storm to which Sarah refers is the battle to save humanity from nuclear holocaust and domination by machines, and it is perfectly clear to the viewer that the dewy-eyed waitress has morphed into a fearless warrior, ready to do whatever it takes to champion humanity. The juxtaposition of Sarah's hairstyle and choice of vehicle with her pregnant state indicates a transgressive bringing together of the supposed opposites of masculinity and femininity. This sets the scene for the sequel, *Terminator 2*, in which Sarah will champion humanity with a combination of feminine and masculine strengths. On the one hand, she will strive to both protect and train her son, so that he will be fit for the possible battle in his own future. On the other hand, the opening scenes of *T2* show Sarah demonstrating a masculine level of strength by performing pull-ups (an exercise that takes great upper body strength, and that is beyond the power of most women). Once again, as in *GI Jane*, a woman takes on a key marker of gender difference: muscular strength.

Indeed, the contrast between the Sarah Connor characters of the first and second *Terminator* films is dramatic. She has lost her curves, replacing them with wiry muscles that give her body and face an androgynous cast. She also has lost her "bubbly" lightness of spirit, and instead has a brooding darkness that occasionally explodes into acts of violence. She has become very much the antithesis of the stereotypically attractive, feminine woman – but she has also become an appropriate embodiment of someone who carries the weight of the world on her shoulders, and who knows that only her own heroism and the heroism she manages to teach her son can save the world and all of its people. Sarah demonstrates an interesting reconciliation of the conflict between the needs of the many and the needs of the few, referred to above in relation to Ripley. Contrary to those who espouse biological determinism, Sarah is not narrowly focused only on her domestic unit – if she were, she would presumably be focused on making a nuclear bomb shelter somewhere in Alaska. Instead, she embraces the responsibility to save the world, in the best heroic tradition of seeing the big picture. However, she also is resolutely focused on the welfare of her son, working indefatigably to avert the nuclear holocaust that will propel him into the horrific role of leader of the fight against the murderous machines. In this she is undeterred by anything; not even the ontological paradox that if the nuclear holocaust unleashed by the machines never occurs, Reece will never be sent back in time to try to avert it, and therefore will not have the opportunity to father Sarah's son, so that the son she is working to protect will not even exist.

As an example of Sarah's acts of physicality and violence, she leaves the men and boys behind in the desert, racing off alone in their stolen station wagon to kill Miles Dyson, the man who is fated to invent Skynet – which in turn will lead to the machines taking over the world. Sarah is neither insane nor a murderer, but she plans to kill Dyson for the greater good. As noted above, this is a characteristic of the traditional male hero, who usually takes social well-being into account, rather than only his own family's well-being, as women are traditionally supposed to do. In this scene Sarah takes on the difficult task of balancing all of these spheres. She plans to murder Dyson to save the world, but leaves her son out of it to spare him the sight of his mother committing murder. In addition, killing Dyson might ultimately spare her son from an extremely unpleasant future. She shoots at Dyson through the window, and misses because he happens to move. She invades the home, but then finds that she cannot finish off the quivering, injured man in front of his wife and child. She has the gun aimed at him, and she says, "It's all your fault, I can't let you do it, I won't let you do it." But then she hesitates, and it is apparent that a great struggle is raging in her head. With both hands clasped around the phallic gun, her "feminine" side comes through.

As Sarah struggles through those long seconds, I suggest that we are witnessing her evolution into a new kind of action hero – a hero who blends the masculine attributes, which have brought her here to save the world singlehandedly, with the feminine qualities of empathy and caring that make it impossible for her to kill an innocent man in front of his family. Instead, her mind races to evolve, to devise a different way to save the world. She sits down, rendered almost catatonic by the struggle. Her son arrives, and she cries in his arms. He is comforting, in a way more often associated with women. Interestingly, John is learning to be a feminine *and* masculine hero from his mother – *not* just a masculine hero. As the new breed of hero, she has more to teach him than just the mechanics of guns and explosives. This suggests another interesting and transformative possibility – that the new way in which women embody heroes will reframe the ways in which men are able to be heroes, by creating new archetypes which make wider gender variations and combinations possible for everyone. On the one hand, Sarah illustrates Halberstam's point that masculinity may be authentically enacted by female-bodied people. On the other hand, her son's response to her illustrates Butler's point that anyone may authentically enact any kind of gender behavior. Ultimately Sarah does not kill Dyson, but instead enlists his help in a collaborative attempt to save the world.

THE NEW FEMALE ACTION HEROES IN RECENT FILMS illustrate many of the points made by gender theorists. They unequivocally demonstrate Halberstam's point that masculinity can be enacted by female-bodied people. They clearly show that people may perform different kinds of gender behaviors, depending on circumstances and personal choices. Thus, they lay to rest the old assumptions of biological essentialism, just as surely as they dispatch aliens, terminators, and other assorted bad guys. Moreover, they adapt speedily and flexibly to changing circumstances, and in this way they illustrate Deleuze's notion of transformativity, becoming a new, emergent system by bringing together two systems – the masculine and the feminine, which thus turn out not to be mutually exclusive, but in fact surprisingly complementary and compatible. The female action heroes of recent filmic texts are "feminine" in that they display maternal instincts and empathetic care. However, they are also "masculine" in that they engage in ways of thought and behavior that have traditionally been considered masculine, such as claiming the right to authority, or displaying strength, courage, assertiveness, leadership, physicality (and sometimes violence), and very often heroism.

Thus, the new female action heroes go beyond traditional heroism, and behave as something entirely new – as female-bodied people who freely choose from a range of hitherto gender-linked behaviors to create a new mix that enables them to be a new kind of hero – a female action hero, not just a woman behaving like the archetypal male action hero. As will be shown in the next chapter, female action heroes on the small screen have been similarly transformative and transgressive, and have in fact expanded the definition of hero even further.

NOTES

1 Ripley bluntly asks Clemens, the prison's Chief Medical Officer, if he is attracted to her, and then immediately has sex with him. He says to her, "You're very direct," and she replies, "I've been out here a long time." This is the only time Ripley is ever seen to be a sexual being, and it is notable that she assumes the "masculine" prerogative of initiating sex.

2 This occurs near the end of *Alien* – but it should be noted that immediately after this brief scene, she puts on a no-nonsense space suit and bravely defeats the monster.

3 Hysteria has long been associated almost exclusively with women. The word refers to emotional instability caused by trauma. A pertinent example would be shrieking in a corner while an alien attacks someone else – as mentioned before, this was the traditional response of women in science fiction films, while the male hero attempted to fight back. The sexist meaning of the word is abundantly clear from its Greek origins, the word *hysterikos*. Hippocrates coined this term to apply to madness and suffocation in women, caused by a lack of sexual intercourse, leading to their uteri becoming too light and travelling upwards to compress vital organs such as the heart and lungs. Various feminists have commented on this word; interestingly, some of them have linked the phenomenon to gender roles. For example, Carroll Smith-Rosenberg suggests that hysteria arose due to intolerable ambivalence towards society's gender roles, and is also an unconscious mechanism which the body can use to resist gender roles. Luce Irigaray argues that Freud never constructed an adequate theory of female sexuality, and that it this lack which allows women to labelled as hysteric (Lukinbeal and Aitken 1998).

4 This neologism refers to a cybernetic organism, a machine cloaked in human flesh, comprising artificial and natural systems. In 1960, Manfred E. Clynes and Nathan S. Kline conceived of an enhanced human being who could live in extraterrestrial environments, and suggested: "For the exogenously extended organizational complex functioning as an integrated homeostatic system unconsciously, we propose the term 'Cyborg'" (Clynes and Kline 1960: 26). More recently, the term "cyborg" has been given much wider exposure in Donna Haraway's "Cyborg Manifesto: Science, Technology, and Socialist-Feminism in the Late Twentieth Century" (1991). Interestingly, Haraway argues that the cyborg is outside gender.

CHAPTER 4

WOMEN HEROES OF THE SMALL SCREEN: BOLDLY GOING WHERE NO WOMEN HAVE GONE BEFORE

ALL OF THE TEXTS I AM EVALUATING FALL INTO THE CATEGORY either of fantasy, or of science fiction. I am treating science fiction as a sub-genre of fantasy, although the relationship between fantasy and science fiction is highly contested – for example, some critics maintain that fantasy may be seen as a sub-genre of science fiction. While it is beyond the scope of this book to attempt to resolve this issue, it is useful to briefly consider the nature of fantasy, as well as the nature of science fiction. Timmerman (1983) suggests that there are six traits which must be present in order for a work to be classified as fantasy literature: "the use of traditional Story, the depiction of Common Characters and Heroism, the evocation of Another World, the employment of Magic and the Supernatural, the revelation of a Struggle between Good and Evil, and the tracing of a

Quest" (4). I suggest that science fiction may be seen as one form of fantasy literature, with the distinction that instead of magic and the supernatural, there is a focus on science and technology (Merrick 2003).

It is significant that the second of the traits of fantasy literature is the depiction of "Common Characters and *Heroism.*" While few find it necessary to state this in definitions, the reality is that heroism is usually enacted by male heroes: the overwhelming majority of heroes in all known literature have been men. The stage was set by Homer's two epic ancient Greek poems, *The Iliad* and *The Odyssey*. The former focuses on the male hero Achilles, and the latter on the male hero Odysseus. These poems are thought to date to around the 8th century BC. Twenty-eight centuries later, the celebrated female writer of fantasy, Ursula le Guin, was still having difficulty imagining a female hero (as discussed in Chapter 1). Moreover, when it comes to science fiction the very nature of the genre has been perceived by many to exclude women altogether, let alone grant them the centre stage as heroes:

> Traditionally, sf [science fiction] has been
> considered a predominantly masculine field
> which, through its focus on science and
> technology, "naturally" excludes women.
> (Merrick 2003: 241).

This assumed exclusion rests on the assumption of a gender binary that is ordained by biology: the biological fact of femaleness is assumed to preclude interest in, or understanding of, science and technology. Given this, it is scarcely surprising to find that the heroes of science fiction stories have overwhelmingly been male. When women have appeared as major characters, they have often been portrayed as nothing but victims of their biology, as for example Rosemary in Ira Levin's *Rosemary's Baby* (1967): Rosemary is used by male controllers to give birth to the (male) anti-Christ, so that she is a victim of both the patriarchy and her own biology.

I T IS ONLY IN RECENT DECADES THAT FEMALE HEROES HAVE begun to emerge, both in literature and in filmic texts. Interestingly in view of the history of science fiction, many of these have appeared in science fiction movies and television shows. As I argued in the previous chapter, female action heroes in recent movies have expanded the concept of the hero, moving it from its traditional, entirely "masculine" position to a new position which also embraces some "feminine" traits, notably maternal feeling. In this chapter, I argue that television has expanded the concept of the hero even further, so that it is in fact possible to speak about a "revisioning" of the archetypal action hero.

Female action heroes have been on television for a long time, in the form of such characters as the titular stars of *Wonder Woman* (1975 – 1979) and *Bionic Woman* (1976 – 1978), and in the form of the crime-fighting women in *Charlie's Angels* (1976 – 1981). However, I contend that all of these women were clearly intended primarily to be objects for what Mulvey (1975) would call the male scopophilic gaze, rather than to be positive role models for ordinary women. Certainly, all of these women seemed to have more "to-be-looked-atness" than autonomous power. For example, the conventionally attractive women in *Charlie's Angels* wore such revealing clothing that the show came to be referred to as "Jiggle

TV" or "T&A TV" (Tits and Ass Television) (Mittelmeier 2007). Lindsay Wagner as Bionic Woman Jaime Sommers was similarly easy on the eyes, and was regularly paired up with Steve Austin, the Six Million Dollar Man. Indeed, the Bionic Woman only exists because of the Six Million Dollar Man's intervention, as it is his pleading that results in her being given bionic limbs; moreover, the two are ultimately married. Thus, the Bionic Woman is in a sense defined by her relationship with a male, just as Charlie's Angels clearly are defined by their relationship with the eponymous Charlie. Tasker (2004:19) summarizes the situation with regard to both the secondary status and the "to-be-looked-atness" of the heroines of these 70s series:

> ... the three investigators who are "Charlie's Angels" were oddly positioned as both fashion plates and action heroines, but also as in the service of the central male figure "Charlie." ... [T]hese series often emphasized the glamorous sexuality of the heroines, an emphasis which sat uneasily with the need to include action sequences.

While all of these women were conventionally beautiful and even glamorous, it is Wonder Woman who most clearly illustrates the "to-be-looked-atness" of these 70s heroines. Firmly in the focus of the scopophilic gaze, Wonder Woman (played by Lynda Carter) deflects bullets with her bracelets, while displaying a classically feminine cleavage, and plenty of thigh above boots that point upwards to her scarcely concealed groin area. The bracelets evoke handcuffs, and the sadomasochistic connotations of these, as well as of the ropes with which she is constantly pictured, have not been lost on many factions of the popular imagination. In general, Wonder Woman has been widely perceived primarily as a sex object. One regular viewer from the 1970s candidly describes his own participation in the scopophilic gaze:

> I tell you any guy that didn't secretly fantasize about seeing Wonder Woman nude when they were growing up is a liar! This *big breasted super hero was so damn sexy in her tiny uniform* I stayed glued to every episode and movie. The sight of her big boobs practically spilling out and that hot ass and long legs were the stuff of dreams! (Sexy Cartoon Porn 2008, my emphasis)

By contrast, Ripley and Sarah Connor are not seen in tiny uniforms that emphasize large breasts, nor do any parts of their bodies "spill out" for the scopophilic gaze. Similarly, the female action heroes of the small screen described in this chapter are notably more modest in their attire – although some of them, such as Buffy the Vampire Slayer, had early episodes that were reminiscent of Wonder Woman and her ilk, as they revealed somewhat more of Sarah Michelle Geller's body than was strictly necessary. On the other hand, this mode of dress was appropriate for a teenager trying to make an impression in her new high school; while Wonder Woman's attire arguably is only appropriate for a stripper trying to make an impression in a new night club. Moreover, as pointed out by Thompson (2003), although feminists have found much to criticize in Buffy's wardrobe because "[i]n the first two seasons, Buffy fought evil dressed mostly in flimsy spaghetti tops and short skirts," nevertheless as the series goes on, her wardrobe matures with her character. Once she becomes a young woman, she abandons the "girly" dress for more appropriate attire, and in "The Gift" (the finale of the 5th season, which was originally intended to be the series finale) she "wears pants and a loose, long sleeved top, giving her greater maneuverability and a more 'masculine' appearance" (Thompson 2003). As so often happens with real life women, Buffy learns over time that "girly" clothes have limited usefulness, and adopts more utilitarian garb as she herself attains greater independence and maturity. Xena Warrior Princess's attire does not change over time, and is anything but modest; however, she too cannot be dismissed as merely an object for the scopophilic gaze, as will be argued further below.

The tendency for heroines on the small screen to serve primarily as sex objects for the scopophilic gaze began to change with *Star Trek Voyager*, which premiered in 1995 and featured the first female captain of a starship. The original Gene Rodenberry series *Star Trek* (1965 – 1969) featured a swaggeringly macho (though likable withal) hero, Captain James T. Kirk, played by William Shatner. The series was remarkable for capturing the hippy Zeitgeist, and daring in featuring a multiracial crew (including the first Asian on prime time TV). But the women, by and large, were 60s sex symbols, and there was not a hero among them.

HOWEVER IT IS NOTEWORTHY THAT *STAR TREK* WON RESPECT for including one of the first black women to appear in a major role on TV – previously, black women on TV had been cast as servants. Nichelle Nichols played communications officer Lieutenant Uhura for many years, and was persuaded by Dr. Martin Luther King Jr. to keep playing the role when she wanted to quit, because he believed she was a vital role model for young black women in the USA (Startrek.com 2006). However, while Uhura played a key technical role, she was definitely secondary in the development of characters and relationships; moreover, she had few if any of the heroic masculine traits here under discussion, and was certainly not an action hero.

It is pertinent to contrast Uhura with a much more recent character: Zoe (played by Gina Torres) in Joss Whedon's short-lived but hugely popular (some would say revered) television show, *Firefly* (Whedon 2002 – 2003). Like Uhura, Zoe is African-American and conventionally beautiful. However, she is not a secondary character. She is one of the strongest and most competent people on the ship, and second-in-command to the captain. She is married to the pilot, Wash (played by Allan Tudyk), and it is he, rather than his wife, who may be seen as similar to Uhura – he plays a key technical role, but is definitely secondary in the development of characters and relationships; moreover, he has few if any of the heroic masculine traits here under discussion, and is certainly not an action hero.

However, his wife Zoe most certainly has all of the heroic masculine traits mentioned in my definition: she claims the right to authority, and displays strength, courage, assertiveness, leadership, physicality (and often violence). Finally, she is most certainly an action hero, and usually fights side-by-side with the captain against the bad guys, using fists, guns or whatever comes to hand. She is a formidable fighter (possibly the most formidable of the entire ensemble), and is frequently referred to as a "warrior." Thus, with the passage of almost four decades, the heroic potential of African-

American women in science fiction shows may be said to have been entirely re-envisioned. This appears to reflect the wider social reality, in that the year 2008 saw the election of an African-American president of the United States – an event that would have been unimaginable in the year 1966, when the first episode of the original *Star Trek* series aired.

Star Trek premiered in 1966, and for almost three decades, the starships of the Federation were captained by heroic, hyper-rational men, who steadfastly put the needs of the many ahead of the needs of the few (although Captain Kirk did have a few shaky moments, particularly when attractive, young women were in the picture). This regard for the greater good may be seen as a key feature of the action hero, and is shared by all of the female action heroes discussed in the previous chapter. But in 1995, the first female captain of a Federation starship strode boldly onto the bridge, in the debut of the fourth *Star Trek* series, *Voyager*. Kate Mulgrew shines as Captain Kathryn Janeway, an aquiline-jawed, deep-voiced, calm and utterly confident leader. Indeed, I argue that Janeway is the first true female action hero of the small screen. As is required of action heroes, she unfailingly demonstrates respect for the greater good, placing the needs of the many above the needs of the few.

When Janeway first appears in the series premier of *Voyager*, "Caretaker," she is standing on the bridge of her starship with her legs spread and her hands on her hips. The camera angles up to her, giving the impression that she is large and tall (although in fact she is neither). She is recruiting people for an important mission, with all the confidence of any male hero. As she takes command, she immediately finds herself confronting vestiges of sexism in the Federation: for example, the protocol is for captains to be called "Sir."

Janeway deals with this problem in her characteristic, head-on way, informing Ensign Harry Kim that she does not like to be called "Sir," that "Ma'am" is acceptable in a crunch, but that she'd prefer "Captain." The bemused young man replies, "Yes Ma'am" – to which Janeway crisply replies, "It's not crunch time yet, Mr. Kim. I'll let you know when."

The appearance of Captain Kathryn Janeway on the deck of the *U.S.S. Voyager* was an extraordinary event in media history. As Inness (1999: 103) points out:

> For many years, the producers of the *Star Trek* shows refused to cast a woman for the captain's position out of fear that their largely male audience would not be able to relate to a woman … When Janeway was finally introduced as a captain, a heated battle raged about how her gender would influence her ability to be a leader.

As Jeff Taylor, co-creator of *Voyager*, comments:

> The most pressing concern about a female captain, of course, is will people buy that she's a captain? Will they accept that a whole crew would follow her, report to her, trust her in battle? This is the most important selling point in a woman. Kate Mulgrew has that without even working at it. As a person, as a human being, she is everything that we envisioned Janeway being. She has power coming out of her genetic code, and the moment that she walked out on that bridge

the first day, she owned it. (Quoted on the
back cover of the Columbia House video of
the series premiere of *Voyager*)

Despite her impressive personal talents, the fact that
Mulgrew was cast as Captain Janeway certainly shows that
the creators of television shows had taken a quantum leap
forward, and were finally able to envisage women as action
heroes and leaders, even in the science fiction genre. This
is extremely significant, especially given that women had at
one time been perceived as precluded from science fiction
altogether by biology (as discussed at the beginning of this
chapter). Television producers must have been influenced by
social realities around them: this was 1995, and Ripley and
Sarah Connor had already enjoyed spectacular success.

Moreover, by 1995 many women had emerged from the
kitchen and entered the public sphere; some had
even made it to the boardroom. As McCaughey
and King (2001) comment, we live in a world in which
middle-class white women comprise an important part of the
paid labour force, so that Barbara Ehrenreich has referred to
the "decline of patriarchy." In this postmodern world, many
women have become economically independent of men, and
most men have given up the charade of providing for and
protecting women: "In this new world, women move away
from the moral (and nonviolent) purity of the Victorian
'Cult of True Womanhood' and onto men's turf ... Such
a culture puts violent women (as heroes or villains) in its
movies" (McCaughey and King 2001: 5).

Perhaps equally important from the point of view of
television producers was the fact that just as many women

as men watched television; this, coupled with their increasing economic prosperity rendered them an important aspect of viewership demographics (as the point of most television is to sell products by attracting viewers, who are then captive audiences for the adverts which punctuate shows). The issue of demographics is explored more fully below.

Star Trek enjoys a massive viewership comprising both female and male viewers of all ages – and all seemed entirely capable of accepting a female captain, judging by the fact that the show ran for six years (1995 to 2001). Moreover, not only was her gender different from preceding heroes; she also was a different kind of hero. Indeed, Janeway illustrates my point that female masculinity and female heroism do not demand the large muscles that the archetypal hero (as epitomized by Schwarzenegger and Stallone) must have. All of the qualities I propose in my definition of female masculinity are relevant to Janeway's behavior:

> … female masculinity … consists in female-bodied persons engaging in *ways of thought and behaviour* that have traditionally been considered masculine, such as claiming the right to authority, or displaying strength, courage, assertiveness, leadership, physicality (and sometimes violence), and very often heroism.

This is precisely what Janeway epitomizes. Her attitude, her thinking and her behavior mark her as "masculine." Unlike the impressively towering Lieutenant Ripley, Captain Janeway is a short woman. She is seldom seen with a weapon, and appears to pose no physical threat to anyone. In this, she is entirely unlike male action heroes. Yet she utterly claims the right to authority from the very first moment that she strides onto the deck – without having to knock people around to do so. As noted by Inness: "Unlike Ripley, Janeway, despite being physically fit, almost never lugs around big guns or flexes her pecs in a t-shirt. Yet, Janeway is still very much a leader, and a tough one" (1999: 103). I argue that Janeway expands the notion of action hero in a way that is crucially important for all women, for she shows that it is unnecessary to compete on a physical level with men in order to be a hero or a leader. Mental and moral strength suffice – and Janeway has these in abundance. Indeed, the foundation for such a hero was laid with previous Star Trek series, notably *Star Trek: The Next Generation*, in which Patrick Stewart as Captain Picard is physically underwhelming, yet morally and intellectually compelling, so that his right to authority and unquestioned leadership is established by his brain, not his brawn. *Voyager* was important in that it took the logical next step in depicting such a hero as a woman.

T WO YEARS AFTER JANEWAY TOOK COMMAND OF THE *U.S.S. Voyager*, television history was made again – this time when a blonde cheerleader arrived to take back the night for women everywhere. *Buffy the Vampire Slayer* was one of the most successful television series ever made, and unlike many other science fiction shows, was welcomed as much by females as by males. Even *Ms.* magazine proclaimed: "Many feminists have been dreaming of mass-culture moments like this since feminism came into being … [and] [n]o woman television character has exhibited the confidence and strength of the male heroes of archetype and fantasy … until now" (Magoulick 2006: 730). It seems that women

were more than ready to see women heroes on television, and
television producers finally were ready to cater to this need.
As noted above, a culture in which tough women appear in
real life will also put tough women onto its television screens.
However, the interesting thing about doing so is that once
women action heroes enter the realm of science fiction and
fantasy, they open up new vistas of possibility for the young
women who view them. As will be discussed further below,
the titular hero of *Buffy the Vampire Slayer* role models aspects
of heroism that can be appropriated by all women, not just
super heroes.

The first episode of *Buffy the Vampire Slayer* set the tone
for the entire series, immediately announcing that this would
be a long-overdue twist on the lengthy succession of science
fiction tales which had relegated women to screaming,
helpless victims in the corner. In the opening scene the
viewer sees a dark, deserted school. The camera is inside
the building. Suddenly, the silence is broken by the sound of
smashing glass, as a window is broken by a young man. A
young blonde woman with him anxiously asks, "Are you sure
this is a good idea?" He tells her firmly: "It's a *great* idea –
now come on." The two climb in through the window. They
are now in the empty corridors of Sunnydale High. The
young man wants them to go onto the roof of the gym, but
the woman is reluctant. The man says lasciviously, "Oh, you
can't wait, huh?" and attempts to kiss her. However, she pulls
away, apparently frightened by a noise. Reluctantly, the young
man humors her, and checks to see that no one else is around.
Then he turns to her and says, "There's nobody here." She
asks nervously, still peering into the dark, "Are you sure?"
and he replies: "Yes, I'm sure." She says, "OK," and then
swings back towards him suddenly, her face transforming

into that of a vampire, as she emits a low but feral growl and sinks her teeth into his neck. He collapses, crying out in pain. The scene then fades to the opening credits, with the shocked viewer well aware that it is not only vampires that will be skewered in this show – gender norms also will be skewered. A young woman has "taken advantage" of a young man, rather than the other way around. Moreover, the viewer's fear for the safety of the young woman turns out to be entirely unwarranted – in this show, women are more likely to be aggressors than victims. In addition, the scene upsets tradition in that vampires are traditionally male fictional characters preying on female victims, not females preying on male victims. The clearly trumpeted message that night is no longer a time when women are in constant danger from male aggressors is reinforced later in the same episode, when a strange man follows a vulnerable-looking, young schoolgirl, Buffy Summers, through dark alleyways. Instead of becoming frightened, she lies in wait for him (by doing a handstand on a pole above head height), and then floors him with a powerful two-footed kick, before demanding to know why he is following her. In this show, women take back the night with a vengeance.

True to the promise of this first show, all seven seasons of *Buffy the Vampire Slayer* depict a female action hero who not only does not have to wait to be rescued, but who repeatedly saves both her friends and the world from all manner of hideous enemies – vampires, miscellaneous demons, and even a giant, shape-shifting female praying mantis (the last-mentioned in one of the less stellar moments of the show). Buffy's creator, Joss Whedon, is a third-generation feminist, as his mother and his grandmother were both active feminists. Following in their footsteps, he succeeds in creating a female action hero who fights back aggressively, instead of running away screaming. Buffy transgresses the gender binary, smashing the stereotype of the helpless female victim, and showing that women can be heroes too. This was precisely Whedon's intention: as noted in Chapter 1, Whedon states: "I saw so many horror movies where there was that blonde girl who would always get herself killed. ... I thought it was time she had a chance to take back the night" (Kuzui and Whedon 1992). However, Buffy is initially a reluctant hero, even though it is her destiny to be a vampire slayer, because as the opening credits of every episode tell us:

> Into every generation a Slayer is born. One
> girl in all the world, a Chosen One. One
> born with the strength and skill to fight the
> vampires, to stop the spread of their evil and
> the swell of their numbers.

THE NOTION THAT IT IS BUFFY'S DESTINY TO SAVE THE WORLD from evil is particularly interesting in view of the biological determinism underlying assertions such as Freud's that "anatomy is destiny." In this, Freud arguably was merely making explicit that which is believed implicitly by all who subscribe to the gender binary, that is, that one's gender determines one's primary personality traits. In response to Freud's pronouncements, Karen Horney suggests that culture rather than biology is the primary determinant of personality, and that it is our culture, not our biology, that prescribes that women should be in an inferior position to men. She argues that if women feel inferior to men, it is not due to penis envy, but rather is a pragmatic response to social realities. As she puts it: "[t]he wish to be a man ... may be the expression of a wish for all those qualities or privileges which in our culture are regarded as masculine, such as strength, courage, independence, success, sexual freedom, right to choose a partner" (1939: 108). It is notable that the first four "masculine" qualities that Horney lists (strength, courage, independence, success) are all associated with male heroes, and that the first two are part of my suggested definition of masculinity. The third, "independence," may be equated with the quality of assertiveness, which is also part of my suggested definition of masculinity. In short, Freud asserts that biology ordains personality, and implies that biology effectively precludes women from heroism. However, Horney makes the point that it is culture rather than biology that precludes women from attributes associated with masculinity (and hence precludes them from heroism, as all of the heroic traits are also assumed to be masculine traits). *Buffy the Vampire Slayer* moves Horney's rebuttal into the popular realm. Indeed, it turns Freud's assertion entirely on its head, suggesting that not only does female anatomy *not* imply a destiny of inferiority, but that female anatomy may go hand in hand with a destiny of heroism and greatness: a destiny to save the world!

In the series premiere of *Buffy the Vampire Slayer*, Buffy resists this destiny. She has already been a slayer for a year, in Los Angeles, and the result was that she had to burn down the school gym in order to vanquish vampires – an act that resulted in her expulsion from school, as only Buffy knew the real reason for her act of arson. She and her mother have moved to Sunnydale as it is the only place that will accept a girl with a school record such as Buffy's.[1] Buffy now hopes for a quiet life, as does her mother. Unfortunately for both of them, Sunnydale is situated on a hell mouth, and their arrival in the town is not coincidental; rather, it is her destiny. Thus she is expected, and a Watcher (Rupert Giles, played with understated style by British actor Anthony Stewart Head) awaits her, to guide her in fulfilling her destiny. Buffy resists, aspiring to be an ordinary teenager and a cheerleader, rather than a vampire slayer. However, she is drawn back to her heroic destiny by the imminent danger posed to her new friend, Willow Rosenberg (played by Alyson Hannigan). Buffy notices a vampire escorting Willow out of the Bronze, a nightclub, and sets off in hot pursuit to save her. Soon two of her other new friends, Xander Harris (played by Nicholas Brendon) and Jesse (who dies so quickly that it is scarcely worth noting who played him), are also in danger, and Buffy is in the thick of mortal vampire combat. From that time forward, she stops resisting her destiny.

THE CRUCIAL POINT HERE IS THAT BUFFY BECOMES AN ACTION hero partly because it is her destiny, and partly out of concern for her friends. Thus, she is not the archetypal lone, macho hero on a public-focused mission to save the world. While she is indeed on a mission to save the world, her motivations lie *both* in the public and the private spheres. Buffy wants to save the world, but on a day-to-day level, she cares about her friends and wants to save *them*. This is important, for it is precisely in regard to how she relates to her friends that Buffy expands, and indeed revisions, the traditional hero archetype. As Ross (2004) succinctly summarizes it, both *Buffy* and *Xena: Warrior Princess*:

> … stress that a woman can be "tough enough" to fight patriarchy when she learns to listen to other women's perspectives on

the world and when she values her emotional
bonds with other females as a source of
strength. ... [As a result, both women] *push
the limits of what it means to be a hero.* (231, my
emphasis)

Ross (2004) points out that both Buffy and Xena talk
with their woman friends in order "to understand how their
experiences are rooted in patriarchy, so that they may take
action to improve their lives as women" (232). Moreover,
this applies to both the titular heroes and their women
friends. Thus, in stark contrast to the archetypal isolated male
action hero, these women construct their heroism within a
community, and are not so much heroes *for* other people as
heroes *with* them:

The lead characters must be strong enough
psychologically and emotionally to *change their
approaches to being heroic*, they learn that the
toughest hero is a flexible one who relies on
others. (Ross 2004: 233, my emphasis).

It is also noteworthy that Buffy values her friendships
with both women *and* men. She immediately becomes
friends with school nerds Willow and Xander, and remains
firm friends with both of them throughout the series (with a
notable interruption when Willow temporarily becomes evil).
In the course of this, she subverts the heroic archetype not
only by gaining power from her friends, but also by *sharing
power* with them. Xander is empowered to work through his
nerd status and find his own relatively modest version of
heroism. This situation of a woman teaching a man how to

become a new action hero is reminiscent of *Terminator 2*, in which Sarah Connor teaches her son John how to be a hero. Similarly, Willow's relationship with Buffy empowers Willow to grow from a bullied computer nerd into a strong, confident (lesbian) woman. She also attains great power as a witch, and at the end of the series plays an essential part in saving the world with her magical powers, thus becoming a female action hero in her own right. This sharing of power between women is reminiscent of *Xena*, where the petite, blonde, and seemingly helpless Gabrielle saves the powerful Xena's life in the very first episode, using her powers of communication and persuasion to rescue her from angry villagers. Again and again, women action heroes show that the traditionally masculine strengths do not suffice on their own: true heroism demands the addition of traditionally feminine strengths.

Read in this way, the series finale of *Buffy* is a triumphant sharing of Buffy's power with the entire world, in which the concept of the action hero is entirely revisioned. Here one must bear in mind the archetype of the action hero as a lone wolf, alienated from the world as he pursues his destiny as a hero. A clear example is Superman, unable ever to marry or even to have close friends because his identity must always be kept a secret, doomed to pine forever for an authentic relationship with Lois Lane. Similarly Batman – apart from his odd and somewhat campy liaison with Robin – lives alone, a man apart, his identity hidden behind a bizarre mask, moving in the shadows as he carries out his heroic feats. In the world of filmic action heroes, one need only think of Rambo, a Vietnam veteran with serious psychological damage, roving alone across the world, shooting some things and blowing up other things.

T IS WITHIN THIS CONTEXT THAT THE SHARING AND CARING exhibited by both Xena and Buffy must be appreciated as a true re-visioning of the action hero archetype. Just as Buffy has her two faithful friends, Xena has her faithful sidekick Gabrielle, who joins her in the very first episode and seldom leaves her side. This is despite the fact that Xena tries very hard at first to shake off Gabrielle, and seems to acquiesce almost reluctantly to the friendship. For example, at the end of Episode 1, "Sins of the Past," Gabrielle arrives at Xena's campfire, having followed her secretly. This dialogue ensues between the two women:

XENA: You know I'm sending you home in the morning.
GABRIELLE: I won't stay home. I don't belong there, Xena.
  I'm not the little girl that my parents wanted me to be.
  You would understand.
XENA: It's not easy proving you're a different person.
  (Reluctantly flings a bedroll at her.) You can sleep over there.
  (They smile at each other.)

Next morning, as the two walk off into the distance:
XENA: You know where I'm headed, there'll be trouble.
GABRIELLE: I know.
XENA: Then why would you want to go into that?
GABRIELLE: That's what friends do – they stand by each
  other when there's trouble.
XENA: All right ... friend.
(End of episode 1)

True to the promise of this conclusion to the first episode, over the course of the ensuing episodes Gabrielle teaches Xena the value of friendship, caring and sharing. It should also be noted that scenes such as the one above are typical of the many scenes in the series that were characterized by clear homosociality and even homoeroticism between Xena and Gabrielle, which led to the show attracting a large contingent of devoted queer viewers. Evidence of the show's social impact appeared in the form of bumper stickers that echoed religious bumper stickers which query "What would Jesus do?" with a much more aggressive question: "What would Xena do?" Thus both Buffy and Xena reflect the archetype of the "sisterhood of women", which allows women to bond together to resist patriarchy. Buffy and Xena bond with other women to resist patriarchy on a symbolic level, as they re-fashion their identities from victims to heroes.

T HIS DEVELOPMENT IN THE PSYCHE OF THE ACTION HERO towards an approach that emphasizes caring, sharing and working together, and in the process empowering all concerned, is taken much further in *Buffy the Vampire Slayer*. In her relationships with her friends, Buffy is repeatedly shown to be flexible in how she approaches the challenges of living on a hell mouth. While Buffy grows increasingly confident as a leader, she never loses touch with the need to listen to the input of friends in formulating her plans. As Willow says in the second episode, "We're a team." Thus, Buffy may be seen as becoming, in the Deleuzian sense, a new kind of hero, one who eschews the lone wolf archetype and who instead is enriched by (and in turn enriches) her friends. I argue that this amounts to incorporating the traditionally feminine talent for communication into the archetype of the hero, thereby expanding the archetype in an original and useful way, and making it all the richer. This is an important part of the revisioning of the action hero, which, I contend, has been achieved by recent filmic female action heroes. One of the essential traits of fantasy listed at the beginning of this chapter is "the tracing of a Quest" (Timmerman 1983: 4). Like male action heroes before them, both Xena and Buffy are on a Quest to protect the innocent from evil. (This pertains to the Struggle between Good and Evil, which, according to Timmerman, is also an essential trait of fantasy.) However, in pursuing this Quest, they also expand the ways in which such a Quest may be traced: they show that this Quest may be a shared Quest, and that in sharing Heroism (another essential trait of fantasy), heroes grow stronger still – while at the same time the "Common Characters" with whom they share the story also grow stronger (Timmerman 1983).

In this regard, it is necessary to rebut a potential protest, namely, that Buffy is controlled by a male Watcher, and thus is in fact merely a victim of patriarchy, rather than an autonomous, assertive action hero. This protest can be dispelled by careful watching of the show. Even in the first season, when Buffy is very young and still coming to her true power, she listens to Giles only when it suits her. For example, when she plans to try out for cheer leading, Giles is appalled, describing it as a cult, which will distract her from her sacred duty. The following interchange ensues:

GILES: As your Watcher, I forbid it.
BUFFY: And you'll be stopping me – *how*?

In this, Buffy alludes to her super powers, which essentially mean that she has the ability to choose exactly what she wants at all times. Notably, Buffy's ability to choose is in keeping with traditional liberal feminism, which aimed at instilling choice for women. Throughout the series, Buffy maintains this freedom to choose, and is anything but in thrall to Giles. In fact, after Giles is replaced by another male Watcher, Wesley Wyndam-Pryce (played by Alexis Denisof), Buffy refuses to accept any semblance of Watcher authority, and breaks with centuries of tradition by becoming an independent slayer. Earlier in the series, when a group of authorities from the Watcher's Council come to Sunnydale to test her, she entirely repudiates their authority over her, which is also a radical break with convention. This group is led by an older, white man, making it clear that the Watcher's Council symbolizes the patriarchal authority to which Buffy never submits.

Buffy never fully submits to external power, meaning that she remains an authentically independent hero. The same may be said of Xena, and it is this unwavering independence that renders Xena's somewhat revealing costumes comparatively insignificant. Moreover, Xena demonstrates throughout the series uncompromising resistance to all attempts to treat her as a sexual object, projecting the message that she dresses as she does for her own convenience, not to turn herself into an object to be looked at or desired.

While Buffy has freedom to choose, an increasingly mature sense of responsibility causes her more often to choose duty over fun as the series progresses. For example, when she goes on a date with a boy, rather than accompanying Giles to a funeral home, Giles is almost killed by vampires. He does not hold her accountable for this – but she holds herself accountable. In this development, Buffy is, in my opinion, a good role model for all young girls (not just future action heroes), because she is able to accept the responsibility that her powers entail. Of course, in Buffy's case her powers are great, and therefore her responsibility is great. This is in fact a recurring motif with male super heroes. For example, arguably the most pivotal line in the entire *Spiderman* film of 2002 occurs when Peter Parker's Uncle Ben says to him: "Remember, with great power comes great responsibility" (Raimi 2002). The assumption of this great responsibility usually marks the beginning of the hero's quest, as he sets off to battle evil in some form or another. With male action heroes, it is customary for this assumption of responsibility to follow the death of a father figure. Examples include Peter Parker and Uncle Ben (Peter only assumes the vigilante mantle of Spiderman after Uncle Ben dies at the hands of a criminal); Superman and his adoptive father Jonathan Kent (the young superman does not leave to become a protector of the innocent in the big city of Metropolis until after the older Kent dies of a heart attack); Bruce Wayne and his father (Wayne begins training to be the vigilante Batman, on a quest to rid Gotham City of crime, after witnessing the murder of his parents by a petty thief); Luke Skywalker and Darth Vader (the young Skywalker cannot rise to his full power until he has killed his evil father); and so on. Unsurprisingly, this assumption of the patriarch's power following his convenient death is not required for female action heroes. However, the assumption of responsibility most certainly is.

While most women do not have great power, the relaxation of patriarchy in our society means that many do have far more power than ever before – and consequently even more responsibility to use that power wisely. In the heroic tradition, responsibility most commonly has to do with a quest to protect the innocent from the malevolent. Traditionally this has always been the responsibility of male heroes. However, Buffy is a female character who exemplifies the heroic tradition of accepting this duty, and rising to it. Crucially, in so doing she follows in the footsteps of her filmic forebears (Ripley and Sarah Connor), making the "tough decision" to put the needs of the many (the world) ahead of the needs of the few (the domestic unit comprising herself and her mother). In so doing, she negates the supposed biological constraints that have barred women from heroism by keeping them narrowly focused on the welfare of their family units rather than on the "bigger picture." This is crucial because being able to act for the sake of the big picture rather than narrow domestic concerns has always been a quintessential heroic quality – Odysseus was certainly not focused on Penelope's needs when he set out to teach the Trojans a lesson.

WHILE BUFFY SMASHES THE ARCHETYPAL HEROIC TRADITION IN the sense that she works within a team, she is nevertheless every inch both a masculine woman and an action hero. Certainly, she epitomizes the qualities I specify in my definition of female masculinity, by engaging in ways of thought and behavior that have traditionally been considered masculine, such as claiming the right to authority, and displaying strength, courage, assertiveness, leadership, physicality (and sometimes violence), and very often heroism. Physicality and violence are part of Buffy's daily repertoire. In the first episode, when she drops her school bag, a pointed stick (for killing vampires) spills out along with her schoolbooks. However, like Janeway, Buffy is constantly motivated by her concern for the greater good, especially as she matures into a young woman. Female action heroes (like male action heroes, but unlike traditional depictions of women which, as noted previously, depict women as constrained by their biology to the domestic sphere) have an eye to the greater good, and make their decisions accordingly. Buffy takes this to its penultimate lengths when she kills her beloved Angel,[2] because he has reverted to his evil former self, Angelus, and now poses a serious threat to the people she loves, and to the world in general. And she takes it to its ultimate lengths when she gives her life to save her sister and the world, at the end of Season Five.[3] This of course is similar to Ripley's self-sacrifice at the end of the third *Alien* film, *Alien 3*, when Ripley hurls herself into boiling lead to destroy the monster incubating inside her body.

While Buffy thus fits comfortably into the traditional heroic archetype, I argue that she is much more than just another stereotypical hero. On the contrary, over the course of the seven seasons of *Buffy the Vampire Slayer*, Buffy evolves from a frightened, hesitant, reluctant young girl into an entirely new kind of hero: as noted above, she works within a community or team, and grows stronger through communicating with others, while at the same time empowering others. Indeed, I argue that Buffy has done more to transform the hero archetype than any of the other filmic female action heroes. This is all the more true because she has also created a face for female masculinity that transgresses the gender binary all the more effectively for being so recognizably feminine (in the traditional sense). As one young woman muses on her blog:

> Why does femininity have to be seen as being in opposition to feminism? There is a certain extent to which women choose to and enjoy presenting themselves as attractive to men, just as men often choose to and enjoy presenting themselves as

desirable to women. …. To berate female heroes … for wearing makeup or dressing in a sexually attractive manner is in fact to masculinise them – to say they can only be a hero if they do not present themselves as feminine. And again, male heroes (compare Hercules and Angel, as the direct counterparts of Xena and Buffy) are also presented in a conventionally attractive, sexualised manner in terms of their "makeup" and attire, but they are not considered to be problematising their heroic nature in so doing. (Two Sides to Nowhere 30 May, 2007)

This is precisely my point. I argue that women need to be free to act in a "masculine" way while at the same time wearing whatever they choose to wear – and if that happens to be lipstick and a cheerleader's outfit, then so be it. On the other hand, women also need to be free to present themselves in any way they see fit, and still be perceived as legitimate heroes. For example, a female hero who chooses to perform a masculine gender role should be considered no less a hero. Unfortunately, such female heroes have not yet appeared in popular culture. The fact that they have not reflects Halberstam's point that there is a cultural imperative "to reduce sexuality to binary systems of gender difference" (Halberstam 1998: 76). Regardless of Butler's 1990 call to stir up "gender trouble," all female heroes to date have stayed quite close to the "correct" side of the prevalent binary system of gender difference. However, it is possible to perceive the androgyny achieved by the likes of Ripley in *Alien 3* as a step in the direction of dismantling this binary system of gender difference.

WHETHER THE CURRENT HETEROSEXIST PATRIARCHY WILL ever allow an entirely masculine-presenting woman to be the hero of a large budget Hollywood film remains to be seen. It seems unlikely, but hope may be found in the sympathetic reception of Brandon Teena (played with Oscar-winning aplomb by Hilary Swank) in the 1999 film *Boys Don't Cry* about a real life female-to-male transsexual (Peirce 1999). Granted that Teena was far more a victim than a hero, it is nevertheless true that he was heroic in daring to subvert the dictates of the gender binary in the rural mid-west of the United States of America. In the filmic realm, *Aliens* includes a butch female character named Private Jenette Vasquez (played by Jeanette Goldstein), a Latino soldier with impressive musculature and a decidedly masculine presentation. When she first appears on camera she is doing pull-ups, an exercise that is strongly male-identified as it requires great upper body strength, and is not possible for most women (just as the female hero of *GI Jane* signals her masculine toughness by doing one-handed push-ups, and just as Sarah Connor signals that she is ready to be a warrior hero when she does pull-ups at the beginning of *Terminator 2*). A male soldier asks her: "Hey Vasquez, have you ever been mistaken for a man?" Scarcely missing a beat in her pull-ups, Vasquez shoots back: "No, have you?" Vasquez is very brave and a good soldier, and her appearance in this film might have signalled acceptance of women heroes actually presenting themselves as physically masculine – if not for the fact that she is the first in the cast to die a horrible death.

Similarly, while Hollywood has featured a number of women presenting as masculine in one way or another, none of these performances can be seen as positive representations of female masculinity, for varying reasons. For example, Beryl

Reid as George in Robert Aldrich's *The Killing of Sister George* (1968) is butch, but she is an unattractive, sadistic monster of a woman; Robin Johnson as Nicky in Alan Moylan's *Times Square* (1980) is an attractive, young butch, but she is also a juvenile delinquent; Gina Gershon in Larry and Andy Wachowski's *Bound* (1996) is an attractive butch, but she is also a petty thief; and Queen Latifah as Cleo Sims in F. Gary Gray's *Set it Off* (1996) is also an attractive butch – but she is a major criminal who ultimately is killed (Halberstam 1998). Even Danny De Vito's children's film *Matilda* (1996) features a school principal, Miss Trunchbull, who resembles the stereotype of the sporty, butch gym teacher – but who is a cruel, sadistic, child abuser. (In this, the film closely follows Roald Dahl's 1988 book of the same name.) Thus, Hollywood seems to be unable to accommodate masculine-appearing women except by demonizing them.

Arguably, this demonization reflects the still prevalent societal condemnation of masculine-presenting women (*GI Jane* notwithstanding). However, I argue that female masculinity has nevertheless made its way into recent popular filmic texts, because masculinity can be performed *with or without* an accompanying masculine physical presentation. In this I refer to masculinity in the sense that I have defined it, that is engaging in ways of thought and behavior that have traditionally been considered masculine, such as claiming the right to authority, or displaying strength, courage, assertiveness, leadership, physicality (and sometimes violence), and very often heroism. There is no dress code for women who wish to perform masculinity defined in this way. This has the potential to be extremely liberatory, for, as I suggested in Chapter 1, it opens the door for women who prefer to conform physically to social mores to lay claim nevertheless to the authoritativeness and power that has traditionally been the domain of men.

Buffy has made it possible to envisage female masculinity in a short, red and white cheerleader's dress. Moreover, in the course of becoming, over and over again, the hero who saves her friends and the world, she evolves into an entirely new kind of hero which, I argue, revisions the traditional hero archetype into a new kind of hero, suitable for modern times when received gender norms are under rigorous scrutiny. In this process, she again and again chooses to perform those aspects of masculine or feminine gender that work best for specific circumstances. In so doing, she creates a heroic archetype that incorporates what are, arguably, the best of both traditionally masculine and traditionally feminine traits. In particular, she broadens the heroic archetype into one that can draw from the traditionally female traits of sharing, empathetic caring, and a talent for communication, so that all of the people around the hero are both empowered and enriched. The new action hero, as epitomized by Buffy, is able seamlessly to integrate "masculine" traits such as strength, action and heroism with "feminine" traits such as caring and sharing, resulting in triumphant, shared accomplishment by all. While *Buffy* began with one lone girl saving the world, the series ends with the message that all good people may pool their respective talents to save the world. Moreover, Buffy is utterly selfless in this sharing of power. This may be illustrated with reference to the series finale.

In the final episode of the series, entitled "Chosen," Buffy and a large, somewhat motley collection of her allies prepare for a final stand against the greatest danger that has ever faced the earth: an evil power referred to as "The First," which is backed by an army of super vampires referred to as *turok han*. Against this formidable force is pitted a group comprising the following:

- ❖ Spike, formerly an evil vampire, a wiry Englishman with platinum hair, who fell in love with Buffy and went off on a successful search for a soul, and who now stands shoulder to shoulder with his erstwhile enemies against the powers of darkness.
- ❖ Principal Wood, the school principal, a tall, handsome, male African American whose vampire slayer mother was killed by Spike.
- ❖ Angel, a traditionally dark and brooding vampire with an entirely non-traditional soul, Buffy's true love, although the two remain ever star-crossed. He has returned to Sunnydale to help with this final effort, and Buffy asks him "What are you doing here?" to which he responds, "Well, not rescuing a damsel in distress, that's for sure." She replies, as she picks up a massive ax, "You know me, not much for the 'damseling'."
- ❖ Willow, Buffy's Jewish, lesbian best friend, who has proven to be a powerful witch, but who now reserves her power only for special occasions — such as saving the world.
- ❖ Xander, now with only one eye due to a clash with the evil force, but still gamely doing his only-human best to help his two very powerful female friends.
- ❖ Anya, a centuries-old former revenge demon who has renounced her immortality, power and revenge itself, out of love for Xander, and who has been

painfully (but with a charming enthusiasm) learning the lesson of how to be human.

❖ Giles, Buffy's former Watcher, a middle-aged Englishman, who has returned from London to help save the world.

❖ Dawn, Buffy's little sister (who was created by magic, rather than by more traditional means). Like Xander, Dawn has no special powers, apart from the courage and confidence that she has acquired from working with her sister and friends in the fight against evil.

❖ A crew of about thirty Slayer "stand-bys" – young women of assorted races and backgrounds who could theoretically become slayers, if the incumbent slayer should herself be slain. According to the mythology of the show, only one girl at a time can be a slayer. When the incumbent slayer dies (usually horribly, due to the nature of the job), the next in line acquires the superhero powers, which have, until that time, lain dormant within her. All of these young women have been "chosen" as possible successors in the vampire slayer line. Usually, they would be unaware of their possible destiny, but Buffy has assembled them in the hope that they can somehow help to defeat the First – even though they do not have superpowers, as she does.

❖ Faith, a slayer who gained her powers when Buffy died for a short while, and who was corrupted by power for a time, but who has now come back from the dark side. Faith is one of the few working-class characters in a primarily middle-class show. Accordingly, her descent to the dark side has been the subject of some scathing commentary by critics who accuse Buffy of reflecting elitist class values. However, Faith entirely redeems herself in the final season, thus arguably rebutting such criticism.

❖ Andrew, an archetypal "nerd" who has reformed his former ways (when he aspired to be a super criminal), and who now throws in his lightweight lot with Buffy's crew.

I list all of these assorted characters because Ross (2004) has argued that in *Buffy the Vampire Slayer*, Buffy and Willow's strength derives from female friendship and solidarity, in that the two women communicate with each other and work together to empower each other and resist patriarchal attempts to separate them from each other. I would agree that female solidarity is enormously important and empowering in the show, and in itself constitutes a revisioning of heroism. However, I argue that *Buffy* goes beyond this: throughout the show, and particularly in this final episode, we see a coming together of *all kinds of people*, not just two women. There is a pooling of both female and male strength, which is appropriate for a show whose hero incorporates both "masculine" and "feminine" strengths.

In this final episode, all of the above characters are in varying stages of despair, as all fear they lack the collective power to defeat the evil force. Therefore, they all expect imminent and horrible death, followed in quick succession by a horrible death for all other human beings. In this darkest hour, Buffy calls them together and addresses them all:

> Right now you're asking yourself what makes
> this different. What makes us anything more
> than a bunch of girls being picked off one

by one? It's true – none of you have the power that Faith and I do. So here's the part where you make a choice. What if you could have that power? Now? In every generation one slayer is born because a bunch of men who died thousands of years ago made up that rule. They were powerful men. *This woman* [pointing to Willow] is more powerful than all of them combined. So I say we change the rule. I say *my* power should be *our* power. Tomorrow, Willow will use the essence of the scythe to change our destiny. From now on, every girl in the world who *might* be a Slayer, *will* be a Slayer. Every girl who *could* have the power, *will* have the power. Can stand up, *will* stand up. Slayers, every one of us. Make your choice. Are you ready to be strong?

Buffy then outlines her plan: Willow will muster all of her massive powers as a witch to confer their superpowers on the potential superheroes now, rather than only after the death of the preceding slayer. Willow confides in her woman lover (one of the potential slayers) that she is afraid that she will not be up to the challenge, and the young woman reminds her: "Buffy believes in you." This reflects one of the most powerful dynamics of the show, a dynamic that begins in the very first episode and continues to the very end: that of Buffy's support and faith in her friend enabling Willow to become a hero in her own right. Moreover, it is notable that Buffy's male friends are not excluded from this potential: by the end of the series, her male friend Xander is also a hero.

THUS, AN IMPORTANT PART OF THIS REVISIONING OF THE HERO archetype is that heroes make heroes of their friends, too. This is entirely different from the traditional heroic archetype, in which the hero is almost by definition alone and exclusive, the lone, male hero whose heroism is highlighted by its very contrast with the comparative weakness of his peers. James Bond is remarkable because other secret agents cannot achieve what he can achieve; Superman is remarkable because he has powers that ordinary men do not have; the heroes of cowboy epics are remarkable and formidable because they shoot straighter, ride faster and hit harder than their peers. None of these heroes has the slightest desire to share his powers with other people, or to empower them in any way; there are no scenes in which these heroes try to teach their skills to other people. In the case of *Buffy*, the message is that even nerdy girls who are picked on by their peers can come into their own power and become heroes – it is not just freakish, exceptional women who may be heroes. Moreover, they can find this power due to the support of their friends who believe in them.

This is a powerfully revisionist dynamic, and seems to be a culmination of what Le Guin set out to do when she attempted to "revision vision" by imagining what a female hero in a fantasy tale might be (Le Guin 1993: 12). To recall Chapter 1, Le Guin argued that "thanks to the revisioning of gender called feminism, we can see the myth [of male heroes] as a myth: a construct, which may be changed; an idea which may be rethought, made more true, more honest" (Le Guin 1993: 17). In envisioning heroes who are not only female but who empower other women to be heroes, and by extension implying that all women have the potential for the very heroism from which they were thought to be precluded by their biological destiny as women, *Buffy* takes the process which Le Guin began to its logical and liberatory conclusion. There are of course two allied forces that have conspired to keep women disempowered: their alleged biological destiny, aided and abetted by a powerful patriarchy that explicitly excludes women from power. Indeed, these forces may be perceived as two sides of the same coin: sexist, patriarchal discourse. I have argued above that Buffy's destiny as a slayer refutes the notion that women's biology implies a limited destiny. In addition, Buffy's final act in the series constitutes a radical revolution against patriarchal power – a revolution that has thus far evoked surprisingly little commentary. In a clear assault on the patriarchy, she decrees an end to centuries-old male prescriptions that severely limit women's power by essentially dividing them – using the age-old method of divide and rule. Buffy empowers *all* potential slayers, and as she does so the camera underlines this by zeroing in on ordinary girls everywhere. The following dialogue ensues:

XANDER: We saved the world.
WILLOW: We changed the world. I can feel them, Buffy. All over. Slayers are awakening everywhere.

In this, *Buffy* has affinities with many feminist texts of speculative fiction, including *The Wanderground* by Sally Miller Gearhart (1985), which asserts the synergistic power of collectivity as opposed to the power of a single exceptional individual. Clearly, when so many women share so much power, control by a tradition-bound, male-dominated Watcher's Council is subverted. In sharing her power, Buffy leads an inexorable charge against traditional, male authority. Thus, the show has grown from its starting point, where a hesitant young woman began to find her power, supported by her two caring friends, to the final, triumphant moment when that same woman, now grown mature, wise and confident, having saved the world with her allies, now in a very real sense passes the torch to all the women of the world by sharing her power with all the potential slayers.

The final episode of *Buffy*, screened in May of 2003, sent a strong message that women are awakening to a new power – more power than women have ever enjoyed before. Moreover, *Buffy* and other shows about women action heroes sent a message that this new power is different from traditional power, for in the course of the past three decades of television history the small screen has seen women action heroes not only don the hero's cape, but actually redesign it. Heroes such as Xena, Janeway and Buffy entirely embody female masculinity, even though none of them looks remotely masculine, reflecting my definition of female masculinity based on behaviors and ways of thinking, rather than on physical appearance.

These female action heroes are able to perform masculinity in a way that is enormously empowering, as the masculine traits and behaviors they choose are those of the archetypal hero: they calmly claim the right to authority, and repeatedly display strength, courage, assertiveness, leadership, and physicality (and sometimes violence). Moreover, these female action heroes also choose to perform many aspects of "femininity" that both increase their power and enrich the archetype of hero, taking it to a place that moves fantasy to an entirely new realm. Indeed, I argue that *Buffy* takes this to the extent that the show may be said to revision the action hero, creating a vision of the action hero that encompasses some qualities of both "masculinity" and "femininity," and thereby modeling a brave new world in which women may choose to perform those gender acts which empower them, rather than being constrained by the narrow dictates of tradition and the patriarchy (or by their allegedly limiting biology).

THIS VISION OF A BRAVE NEW WORLD OF CHOICE IN GENDER performance takes the long-standing feminist demand for women to have freedom to choose to an entirely new level, for it implies that women can not only choose to be equal to men, but also can choose to be as masculine as some men. Here it is pertinent to note that part of the male backlash against the first wave of feminism was an accusation that women were "trying to be like men." To that, an appropriate response might be, "Why not?" Just as a Christian once posed the question, "Why should the devil have all the nice songs?" postmodern feminists may ask, "Why should men have all the heroic qualities?" These small screen heroes effectively demonstrate that – contrary to commonplace assumptions – women can also have heroic qualities. Moreover, they demonstrate that the masculinity traditionally associated with heroic qualities is possible and desirable within female bodies, regardless of what Halberstam refers to as the "collective failure to imagine and ratify the masculinity produced by, for, and within women" (Halberstam 1998: 15). As noted by Halberstam, "female masculinities are framed as the rejected scraps of dominant masculinity in order that male masculinity may appear to be the real thing" (Halberstam 1998: 1). However, these female heroes give the lie to this, for their female masculinities are indeed the real thing – the thing of which extraordinarily successful television series are made, which in turn illustrates that the collective imagination of popular culture is increasingly able to imagine and ratify the masculinity produced by, for, and within women.

I REFER HERE TO POPULAR CULTURE IN GENERAL, BECAUSE contrary to what might be expected, these shows are not only watched by females, or only by adolescent males. For a start, they have enjoyed phenomenal success with both sexes. But beyond that, the demographic that watches these shows is not limited to adolescents. Certainly, shows such as *Buffy* originally targeted young people. However, they targeted them with an explicit sociological intent:

> In this era of postfeminism, new avenues
> are being sought to spread the ideals of
> feminism and the potential of possible
> vehicles, such as mass media, are being
> realised. However, when using mass media,
> such as television, in such a fashion,
> the intellectualizations of the highbrow
> modernist/feminist movements have been
> largely stripped away, leaving little but an
> easily digestible skeletal foundation. The
> aim of such a method is to target a younger
> demographic than traditional critique would
> usually focus upon. The television program
> *Buffy the Vampire Slayer* is such a vehicle,
> presenting feminism in a postmodern form
> "for the masses." (Thompson 2003)

In short, shows such as *Buffy* repackage feminism in a form accessible to non-intellectuals and youth. *Buffy's* creator, Joss Whedon, says of the show, "if I can make teenage boys comfortable with a girl who takes charge of a situation without their knowing what's happening, it's better than sitting down and selling them on feminism" (Fudge 1999:4). Shows such as *Buffy* were aimed at young people and certainly reached this target, along with their message of feminism – packaged for a postmodern era.

However, it is pertinent to note that *Buffy the Vampire Slayer* also reached many beyond this target demographic. For example, statistics show that the average age of viewers who watch *Buffy* is 29 (Dumars 1999). This crossing of lines between youth and maturity may be seen as characteristic of the fantasy genre: "In Fantasy, the boundary between childhood and maturity can often become blurred. Stories written for children often examine adult problems in the guise of odysseys through imaginary lands or conflicts with extra-terrestrials" (Cawthorn and Moorcock 1988: 179). It would seem that Buffy was not just a role model and a source of inspiration for adolescents: she appealed also to older viewers. For example, the WB network (which aired *Buffy* in 1999) reported that *Buffy* was its top-rated program in all of these demographics:

❖ Adults 18-34
❖ Women 18-34
❖ Persons 12-34

Buffy also tied with Angel (a program which was a spin-off from Buffy, but which featured a male action hero) as the highest rated series in the following demographics:

❖ Teens 12-17
❖ Male teens
❖ Men 18-49

(Time Warner, December 2, 1999)

These statistics indicate that the post-modernist feminist message of *Buffy* reached a broad swath of society. Moreover, the television shows of the past three decades, some of which I have discussed in this chapter, as well as the filmic texts I discussed in Chapter 3, did more than deliver an accessible message of female empowerment. They also did something quite radical and extraordinary to an archetype that had endured for at least twenty-eight centuries, as will be discussed in Chapter 5.

NOTES

1 The viewer later realizes that the school has lost so many students to vampires that it can scarcely afford to be selective about new students.

2 Angel is Buffy's boyfriend, a centuries-old vampire who has been "cursed" with a soul, and who now roams the earth eternally, attempting to atone for the misdeeds he committed when he had no soul, by fighting his own kind – vampires.

3 This was supposed to be the end of the show, but Buffy's death evoked such a collective howl of outrage and disappointment from her largely North American fans that the producers capitulated and resurrected both Buffy and the show for a further two seasons. This turned out to be salutary, as Season 6 takes the show to its darkest depths when Buffy flirts with BDSM with Spike, a vampire, while Season 7 saw the show soar to new heights in terms of revisioning the heroic archetype, as is discussed further below.

CHAPTER 5

CONCLUSION:
A LIBERATORY NEW
ACTION HERO FOR ALL

I N THE LAST THREE DECADES WE HAVE WITNESSED THE SUDDEN
and thrilling emergence of female action heroes with
decidedly masculine behaviors and ways of thinking.
These women have risen to prominence not in a separate
realm or genre, but within the mainstream of action films
and science fiction television. As noted by Tasker:

> ... those action films in which women have taken
> central roles were not developed in a separate
> generic space. Indeed, the increased inclusion of
> women in action roles has both contributed to
> and been part of the ways in which the genre has
> evolved in recent years .... (2004: 68)

Specifically, I suggest that the contribution of female
action heroes in recent filmic texts has been to revision the

age-old archetype of the hero dramatically, moving it from its traditional, entirely "masculine" position, to a new position which also embraces some "feminine" traits, notably maternal feeling and nurturing, empathetic caring, sharing, and a talent for and enjoyment of communication. This position has showcased a new type of heroism, in which heroes share their power, and in so doing empower other people to be heroes, or at least to rise to their fullest potential. This has been achieved by transgressing the boundaries of the old heroic archetype in no uncertain terms, thereby transforming it into a new archetype that embraces behaviors and ways of thinking which arguably reflect the best and most positive aspects of both sides of the previously diametrically opposed gender binary. The new female action heroes have in effect offered "an articulation of gender and sexuality that foregrounds a combination of conventionally masculine and feminine elements" (Tasker 2004: 68). In the process, they have given the lie to the claims of biological essentialism by smashing the stereotypes associated with the gender binary; they have convincingly delivered gender performances that were previously thought to be a contradiction in terms, namely, they have performed as masculine women. In doing this, they have asserted the right to perform some of the most powerful and admirable of the traditionally masculine behaviors.

Female action heroes have not simply given up "feminine" performances in favour of "masculine" performances, thus crossing from one side of the gender binary to the other. Rather, they have been truly transgressive, in that they have treated the previously strictly separated behaviors and ways of thinking not as diametrically opposed and mutually exclusive opposites, but rather as a giant smorgasbord of exciting and useful possibilities, from which they have freely chosen whichever behaviors seem appropriate for given situations. In so doing they have taken what are arguably the best parts of femininity and masculinity, and forged them into a type of toughness that has never been seen before, and which transgressively incorporates the realms of femininity and masculinity. Thus, these female action heroes are engaged in a dynamic process of becoming, as they flexibly and freely choose from a range of hitherto gender-linked behaviors to create a new mix that enables them to be an entirely new kind of hero. For example, Ripley's gender expression is more transgressive than if she were merely "acting like a man." Instead, she is acting like – and becoming – something entirely new: a female-bodied person who is able to choose from a range of behaviors linked to both "femininity" and "masculinity." Unsurprisingly for students of Halberstam or Butler, in performing this transgressive range of behaviors, heroes such as Ripley are entirely authentic, and these female action heroes have thus set an exciting and liberatory example for all people, by demonstrating that authentic gender-linked behavior derives from choice, not from biology.

THIS PHENOMENON HAS TAKEN THE FEMINIST DEMAND FOR freedom of choice for women to new levels, for it represents the freedom to choose *how to be*, rather than merely *what to do*. It also has exposed the instability of the gender binary system that was formerly assumed to be cast in biological stone, so that women were thought to be forever precluded, by their very biology, from many powerful and heroic ways of thinking and behaving. Crucially, the possibility for heroism is not limited to extraordinary situations and super-heroic women. Instead, by pointing to the "instability of a gendered system," the new female action heroes have also helped to produce "an alternative space through that instability" (Tasker 2004: 69), so that in fact female action heroes in recent popular filmic texts are blazing the path to a new future of possibilities for women:

> Xena ... and other tough women ... are shaking up women's roles beyond American popular culture. Such figures ... show their female audience members that they can challenge generations-old stereotypes about what it means to be a woman. For centuries, women have been taught to be physically and mentally nonaggressive if they wish to be accepted by society. They were also expected to wait for men to save them. Now, the media's tough women are teaching real women dramatically different ideas about what it means to be female. For example, being aggressive is desirable, and women should not wait for men to save them. Such changing celluloid notions about what it means to be a woman are influencing real life. We have yet to discover in this new millennium where these new notions will take us. (Inness 2004: 15)

We have yet to discover where this revisioning of what it means to be a woman, and the concomitant revisioning of what an action hero can look like, will take us. However, what is clear is that the world has changed, in a way that must surely threaten and ultimately destabilize the patriarchy, for these filmic texts have inevitably spilt over into popular culture. For example, the "Terminator 2: 3-D Interactive Ride/ Show" at Universal Studios in California is a spin-off from the hugely successful *Terminator* films. The entire spectacle is led and dominated by a woman playing the character Sarah Connor. The John Connor character, and even the large bulk of the Terminator character, are mere adjuncts to the central presence of this action hero on a mission to save the world – a hero who is a woman. Thousands of little girls witness this spectacle. Yet when their own mothers were children, just a few decades ago, popular culture was peopled entirely by male heroes, such as Superman, Batman, Spiderman, Aquaman, and the Flash.

IT IS BECOMING INCREASINGLY CLEAR THAT THE BEHAVIORS and ways of thinking commonly lumped together and designated "masculine" may have nothing to do with biology at all; clearly they are, at least in part, societal constructs, most likely constructed to perpetuate a hegemonic system of patriarchy, considering that the "masculine" attributes are precisely those which are required for power in the public sphere. The fact that it is popular culture that is pointing the way to a deconstruction of the supposedly essential construction of masculinity built upon the foundation of male bodies implies that we are edging closer to a more equitable society. Girls now are growing up in a world where women are heroes, both on and off the screen. The most powerful country in the world, the United States of America, recently came close to having a woman presiding over its highest office; moreover, the USA will soon have the imposing Hilary Clinton in the powerful position of Secretary of State. In this, she will follow in the footsteps of

Condoleezza Rice, who is not only a woman but also black (and hence the inheritor of intersecting oppressions). As noted by Inness (2004: 3), "Tough women are appearing not only in the popular media but in real life, too." Surely this will make a difference in the way the girls and young women of today envisage their own femininity, and in the scope they can imagine for their own gender expression in the world.

I SUGGEST THAT THERE IS STILL A CRUCIAL STEP THAT NEEDS TO BE taken: we need to transcend what Halberstam insightfully identifies as the "collective failure to imagine and ratify the masculinity produced by, for, and within women" (1998: 15). Our society venerates many of the attributes associated with masculinity, and these are precisely the attributes that open the way to autonomy and power within the domestic sphere, and more especially within the public sphere. Yet these attributes are routinely denied to half of our children, by actively discouraging them. Hence, it is time to allow our girl children and young women to aspire to female masculinity, as I define it in this book:

> Female masculinity is a particular expression or performance of masculinity, an expression or performance that is entirely authentic, and that consists in female-bodied persons engaging in ways of thought and behaviour that have traditionally been considered masculine, such as claiming the right to authority, or displaying strength, courage, assertiveness, leadership, physicality (and sometimes violence), and very often heroism.

The importance of the freedom to be "masculine" in this sense cannot be over-stated, for this is a freedom that enables women to escape their frequently assigned prison of the merely domestic, and to be powerful also in the public sphere (whether as heroes or in other ways), where they may act for the good of the many as well as (or instead of) for the good of the few (that is, usually their own domestic circle). Already, millions of real life women engage in such ways of thought and behavior – popular filmic texts do not after all originate from a vacuum, neither are they projected into empty space. However, there is currently an almost schizophrenic conceptual split within the popular consciousness, in that masculine-acting female action heroes are admired on the popular screen, but masculine women in everyday life are repudiated as "unnatural."

In particular, while masculinity in terms of *behavior* and ways of thinking is sometimes condoned (as for example in the cases of Clinton and Rice), masculinity in terms of presentation (dress, hairstyle, and so on) continues to be regarded as unnatural or even pathological. This is very likely the reason why most of the female action heroes I have discussed present as conventionally feminine in terms of their dress and hairstyles. This is salutary on the one hand, because it has the liberatory implication that women who choose to present themselves in a traditionally feminine manner can nevertheless lay claim to behaviors and ways of thinking that have traditionally been reserved for men. Thus, even women who prefer to conform physically to social mores may lay claim to the authoritativeness and power that has traditionally been the domain of men. On the other hand, there is cause for concern in the realization that the gender binary is still maintained so rigidly when it comes to physical attributes, specifically the presentation of the self in terms of aspects such as hair styles and dress.

In this respect, we appear to have advanced little since the days of Radclyffe Hall, when gender performances associated with the "opposite" sex were assumed to be signs of congenital inversion – indeed, judging by the murder of Brandon Teena in 1993, some of us have not advanced at all. Teena (who was born Teena Renae Brandon on December 12, 1972) was a transgendered person, who was born with a female body, but began to live as a male in his teens. When he was just 21, Teena was brutally raped and beaten, then subsequently shot to death, by two men who did not believe Teena had the right to live as a man while biologically a female. The murder occurred in Nebraska, USA, in 1993. The murderers were so filled with hatred that they continued to stab Teena long after he was dead.

This tragedy was a classic example of how strongly some people in our society feel about enforcing rigid gender roles (Jones 1996).[1] Thus, it might be argued that in a very important respect the politically-motivated, hegemonic ideology of the supposedly biologically-ordained gender binary remains salient. Acknowledging the authenticity, legitimacy and respectability of female masculinity (whether physical or psychological) would remove the need that many women still feel to adopt the kinds of masquerades of femininity to which Riviere referred almost 80 years ago. This need is not generated from an unresolved Electra Complex with their mother, but from the fact that most human beings need social approval to legitimate their behaviors. It is time to legitimate female masculinity, so that the door is opened for more female heroes of all kinds and presentations, both on the small and large screens and, more importantly, in real life.

ORTUNATELY THE STAGE IS SET FOR LEGITIMATION OF FEMALE masculinity in this postmodern era, when gender norms are staggering under the weight of rigorous and unremitting scrutiny – from all sides. Indeed, there has been a fascinating congruence between popular culture and sophisticated gender theory, in that both, in their own ways, have attacked the gender binary. Theorists such as Halberstam and Butler have done this explicitly, while films such as the *Alien* series and *Terminator 2* have implied the demise of traditional gender norms by featuring women who boldly transgress them. Similarly, when the producers of *Star Trek Voyager* dared to place their faith in Captain Kathryn Janeway, a loud and clear message was sent that viewers were simply going to have to accept that a woman could captain a star ship. And in the words of producer Joss Whedon, the film and television versions of *Buffy the Vampire Slayer* were about "the joy of female power: having it, using it, sharing it" (Gottlieb 2002).

Concomitantly, in the social sphere, oppressed groups such as gays and lesbians were demanding the exact same privileges accorded to all other human beings, up to and including marriage. While queers were uncompromisingly chanting, "We're here, we're queer, get used to it," *Voyager* effectively – and just as uncompromisingly – said to mainstream audiences, "Yes, the captain is a woman – deal with it." At the same time, Butler (1998) was uncompromisingly calling for gender trouble in order to "open up the field of possibility for gender" (vii) so that people who had hitherto had to "live in the social world as what is impossible, illegible, unrealizable, unreal and illegitimate" (vii) could be recognized as possible, legible, realizable, real and legitimate. In a more narrowly focused but equally important and uncompromising way, Halberstam was demanding the recognition of female masculinity, so that "the masculinity produced by, for, and within women" could be imagined and ratified by the collective imagination (Halberstam 1998: 15).

As I argued previously, the emergence of the notion of women as action heroes was made possible by a profound shift in consciousness which rendered such a notion conceivable: we have evolved to the point where the popular consciousness, the popular media, and also gender theory are able to conceive of masculine, heroic women. This seems to be the result of several combined forces (emanating from the spheres of academia, society and the mainstream mass media), all coming together in an unprecedented but serendipitous way, so that gender and its associated performances are increasingly understood as social constructs, rather than as biologically ordained (and hence immutable) imperatives. Moreover, I contend that the popular filmic texts I have discussed perform an especially valuable function, in that they package a revolutionary, liberatory feminist message in an accessible form. This is salutary, and indeed vitally important. After all, Butler's ideas may be revolutionary, but they are also couched in language that is inaccessible to most people. Halberstam is more accessible, but still is not read by the average adolescent. It is up to popular culture to reach "everyperson", for as pointed out by Inness, "Popular culture does not simply reflect women's lives; it helps to create them …" (Inness 1999: 7).

The average adolescent (and also, as we have seen, older people), were certainly listening when Buffy challenged young women: "Are you ready to be strong?" (final episode of *Buffy the Vampire Slayer*). It seems that women are indeed ready to be strong; they have spent enough time "cowering in corners" and screaming. Indeed, if a contemporary science fiction movie portrayed a women screaming and cowering in the corner while her male friend was beaten to a bloody pulp by an unfriendly alien, the audience would wonder "What's wrong with her?", rather than assuming that her hysterical and cowardly behavior was simply the inevitable result of her flawed, feminine biology. Recalling the triumphant moment when Sarah Connor tells the monstrous terminator cyborg, "You're terminated, fucker," popular culture is effectively proclaiming that the biological essentialism that once consigned women to a weak, inferior status has been terminated.

CONTRARY TO FREUD'S ASSERTION THAT ANATOMY IS DESTINY, popular culture now asserts that anatomy does not dictate destiny, and that women are free to be strong, masculine heros. The *Terminator* films make this explicit: "The future is not set. There is no fate but what we make for ourselves." For women, the message is clear: women are no longer constrained by a biological essentialism which effectively precludes them from all kinds of things, ranging from understanding or enjoying science and technology, to being brave, strong, assertive and physical, to being efficacious in the public sphere, and even to being heroes. Instead, women are now free to choose freely and flexibly from behaviors and ways of thinking considered "feminine" *or* "masculine," so that they can change their own fates, and so that they can be heroes if they choose – thereby saving themselves, and possibly even saving the world! Women can claim the right to authority over not just themselves, but even over the world, if they so choose. The process to which De Beauvoir referred as becoming a woman has become far more open-ended, for the gender-related performances associated with it have become so much more diverse, now encompassing both "feminine" and "masculine" behaviors and ways of thinking. There is tremendous liberatory and transformative potential for *all* women in this new potential for blending all that is best in masculinity and femininity. Indeed, there is tremendous liberatory and transformative potential for all *people* in the acknowledgement that gender performances may be as multifaceted as the weather, and that none of them is less authentic than another – as Butler explained, *all* gender positions are constructed. This leaves the field wide open for all people to construct whatever kinds of gender position they choose, including choosing to be heroes in their own sphere of life.

I suggest that we are witnessing in several parallel and mutually supportive spheres no less than a Copernican revolution in terms of the choices in gender performances that are available to women today. Moreover, there has also been no less than a Copernican revolution in the realm of popular media. While people thought they were simply going to the movies, or relaxing in front of the TV, something extraordinary, even revolutionary, was in fact happening on entertainment screens. The heroic archetype that was already evident twenty-eight centuries ago when Homer wrote about the adventures of Achilles and Odysseus was being attacked and dispatched – terminated, in fact. This archetype had been unassailable for millennia, and almost the entire canon of Western literature had faithfully adhered to it. Accordingly, Jung identified the hero as a key archetype. Yet, as pointed out by Le Guin, this Jungian archetype was an example of "mind forms of the Western European psyche as perceived by a man" (1993: 6). Thus, when it came to contemporary popular culture, all action heroes were male, and there simply were no female heroes. And although the word "heroine" existed, it emphatically was *not* coterminous with "hero." Action heroes were narrowly constrained to a group of behaviors and ways of thinking defined as "masculine," and assumed to be biologically ordained – that is, male action heroes had to have masculine traits because they were males, and heroes had to be male because only masculine traits are heroic. Hence, despite a yawning gap of twenty-eight centuries, there was little difference between Achilles and Clint Eastwood – both of these classic heroic archetypes claimed the right to authority, and displayed (in terms of my definition of masculinity) strength, courage, assertiveness, leadership, physicality (and sometimes violence), and very often heroism. At the same time, both Achilles and Clint showed no talent for communication, little or no regard for family or community, and no interest in sharing or empathetic caring. By contrast, the new female action hero combines all of these with many or all of the classic, masculine heroic ways of thinking.

I conclude that it is impossible to overstate what has happened here – this is no less than a Copernican revolution of the classic heroic archetype. To use Le Guin's term, vision has been revisioned, thanks to the "revisioning of gender called feminism" (Le Guin 1993: 17), and to a serendipitous confluence of popular culture and gender theory. Hence, the old archetype is dead, and heroes will never be the same again. Finally, it is likely that this revolution will impact not only female action heroes, but also male action heroes. There is a moment in *Terminator 2* (which I discussed in Chapter 3) when Sarah Connor breaks down and her son comes to her rescue. Sarah has been rendered catatonic by the conflicting demands of the many and the few, and while her "masculine" side urges her to kill an innocent man, her "feminine" side precludes this. In coming to her aid, her son demonstrates the classic "feminine" attributes of empathetic caring. Moreover, unlike classic male heroes, he is adamant that the needs of the few cannot be sacrificed to the needs of the many – he will not condone the murder of an innocent man, especially in front of the man's wife and child. It thus seems likely that although John Connor may be fated to save the world, he will do so treading not in the footsteps of Achilles, but in the footsteps of his mother, who models the new heroic archetype by combining masculine and feminine behaviors and ways of thinking. Like all of the new female action heroes, Sarah Connor models this new heroic archetype not just for her son, but for everyone, most especially the women and girls of the world.

NOTES

1 Teena's short life and brutal death were the subject of the film, *Boys Don't Cry*, starring Hilary Swank as Teena (Peirce 1999). Swank won an Academy Award for her remarkable performance.

BIBLIOGRAPHY

ATWOOD, MARGARET. 1988; rpt. 1999. *Cat's Eye*. Toronto: Seal Books.

AUERBACH, NINA. 2001. "Waiting Together: Pride and Prejudice". In *Pride and Prejudice*, Donald Gray. (Ed.) 3rd ed. New York: W.W. Norton & Company: 326-338.

AUSTEN, JANE. 1818; rpt. 1996. *Northanger Abbey*. New York: Quality Paperback Book Club.

BARBER, KATHERINE (ED). 1998. *The Canadian Oxford Dictionary*. Toronto: Oxford University Press.

BEESLEY, MARK AND ERIC BREVIG. (Directors). 1995. *Xena Warrior Princess*. MCA Television.

BERGER, MAURICE, BRIAN WALLIS, AND SIMON WATSON (EDS.), 1995. *Constructing Masculinity*. New York: Routledge.

BESSON, LUC. (Director). 1990. *Nikita*. Gaumont.

BONNIÈRE, RENÉ, AND CHRIS GROSS. (Director). 1997. *La Femme Nikita*.

BORNSTEIN, KATE. 1995. *Gender Outlaw: On Men, Women and the Rest of Us*. New York: Random House.

---. 1998. *My Gender Workbook: How to Become a Real Man, a*

Real Woman, the Real You, or Something Else Entirely. New York: Routledge.

BROWN, JEFFREY A. 2004. "Gender, Sexuality, and Toughness: The Bad Girls of Action Film and Comic Books." *Action Chicks: New Images of Tough Women in Popular Culture*. Sherrie A. Inness (Ed.), New York: Palgrave Macmillan: 47-74.

BULLOCK, ALAN AND STEPHEN TROMBLEY. 1999. *The New Fontana Dictionary of Modern Thought*. 3rd edition. London: HarperCollins.

BUNDTZEN, LYNDA K. 1987. "Monstrous Mothers: Medusa, Grendel and Now Alien." *Film Quarterly* 40(3): 11-17.

BUTLER, JUDITH. 1990. *Gender Trouble: Feminism and the Subversion of Identity*. New York: Routledge.

---. 1998. "Introduction: Rethinking Genders." *Velvet Light Trap*, 41: 2-10.

---. 2004. *Undoing Gender*. New York and London: Routledge.

CALIFIA, PATRICK. 2003. *Sex Changes: The Politics of Transgender Politics*. San Francisco: Cleis Press.

CAMERON, JAMES. (Director). 1984. *Terminator*. Hemdale Film.

---. (Director). 1986. *Aliens*. Twentieth Century Fox.

---. 1991. *Terminator 2: Judgement Day*. Twentieth Century Fox.

CAMPBELL, JOSEPH. 1949. *The Hero with a Thousand Faces*. Princeton: Princeton University Press.

CAWTHORN, JAMES AND MICHAEL MOORCOCK. 1988. *Fantasy: The 100 Best Books*. London: Xanadu Publications.

CLYNES, MANFRED E., and Nathan S. Kline. September 1960 "Cyborgs and space." *Astronautics*. 26-27 and 74-75. Reprinted in Gray, Mentor, and Figueroa-Sarriera, eds.

1995. *The Cyborg Handbook*, New York: Routledge: 29-34.

COAKLEY, JAY AND PETER DONNELLY. 2004. *Sports in Society: Issues and Controversies*. Toronto: McGraw-Hill Ryerson.

CROMWELL, JASON. 1999. *Transmen and FTMs: Identities, Bodies, Genders and Sexualities*. Urbana and Chicago: University of Illinois Press.

CROW, BARBARA A. and Gotell, Lise. 2000. *Open Boundaries: A Canadian Women's Studies Reader*. Toronto: Prentice-Hall Canada Inc.

DE BEAUVOIR, SIMONE. 1974. *The Second Sex*. New York: Virago Books.

DE VITO, DANNY. (Director). 1996. *Matilda*. TriStar Pictures.

DELEUZE, G. and F. Guattari. 1987. *A Thousand Plateaus: Capitalism and Schizophrenia*. Trans. Brian Massumi. University of Minnesota Press, Minneapolis.

DUMARS, DENISE. October 28, 1999. "Buffy the Vampire Slayer: Authors Nancy Holder and Christopher Golden." Retrieved 28 Dec. 2006 from http://www.mania.com/buffy-vampire-slayer-authors-nancy-holder-christopher-golden_article_2925.html

DURKHEIM, EMILE. 1999. *The Rules of Sociological Method*. 8th ed. Translated by Solovay, Sarah A. and John H. Mueller, and edited by Catlin, George E.G. New York: The Free Press.

EAGLETON, TERRY. 2004. *After Theory*. London: Penguin.

---. 2003. *Literary Theory: An Introduction*. 2nd edition. Minnesota: University of Minnesota Press.

EARLY, FRANCES H. Winter, 2001. "Staking her Claim: Buffy the Vampire Slayer as Transgressive Woman Warrior." *Journal of Popular Culture*, 35(3): 11- 27.

EDWARDS, TIM. 2004. "Queer Fears: Against the Cultural Turn." *Sexualities*, 1(4): 471-484.

Epstein, Rob and Jeffrey Freeman. (Directors). 1995. *The Celluloid Closet*. Home Box Office.

Fausto-Sterling, Ann. 1992. *Myths of Gender: Biological Theories about Women and Men*. New York: Basic Books.

---. March – April, 1993. "The Five Sexes: Why Male and Female are not Enough." *The Sciences*: 20-25.

---. 1999. "Is Gender Essential?" *Sissies & Tomboys: Gender Nonconformity & Homosexual Childhood*. Matthew Rottnek (Ed.). New York: New York University Press: 52-57.

---. 2000. *Sexing the Body: Gender Politics and the Construction of Sexuality*. New York: Basic Books.

---. 2004. "The Five Sexes, Revisited." *Feminisms and Womanisms: A Women's Studies Reader*. Althea Prince and Susan Silva-Wayne (Eds.). Toronto: Women's Press: 133-138.

---. 1996. *Transgender Warriors: Making History from Joan of Arc to Dennis Rodman*. New York: Beacon Press.

Feinberg, Leslie. 2003. *Stone Butch Blues*. New York: Alyson Books.

Ferraro, Julian. Nov. 22, 1996. "Male-Female Experiences." *Times Literary Supplement*, 4886: 24.

Fincher, David. (Director) 1992. *Alien 3*. Twentieth Century Fox.

Foucault, Michel. 1990. *The History of Sexuality: Volume 1: An Introduction*. New York, Vintage Books.

Freeman, R. and Freeman, T. 1992. "An Anatomical Commentary on the Concept of Infantile Oral Sadism." *Int. J. Psycho-Anal.*, 73: 343-348.

Friedman, Sandra Susan. 1997. *When Girls Feel Fat: Helping Girls through Adolescence*. Toronto: HarperCollins.

Frost, Corey. 2005. "Intersections of Gender and Ethnic Performativity in Ann-Marie MacDonald's Fall on Your

Knees." *Canadian Review of American Studies* 35(2): 195-206.

FUDGE, RACHEL. Summer 1999. "The Buffy Effect: A Tale of Cleavage and Marketing." *Bitch Magazine* 10: 1-10.

GARBER, MARJORIE. 1989. "Spare Parts: The Surgical Construction of Gender." *Differences: A Journal of Feminist Cultural Studies* 1(3): 137-159.

GARDINER, JUDITH KEGAN. "On Female Identity and Writing by Women." In Elizabeth Abel (Ed.) *Writing and Sexual Difference*. Chicago: University of Chicago Press, 1982, pp. 177-91

GEARHART, SALLY MILLE. 1985. *The Wanderground: Stories of the Hill Women*. London: The Women's Press.

GOLDMAN, MARLENE. 1990. "Penning in the Bodies: The Construction of Gendered Subjects in Alice Munro's Boys and Girls." *Studies in Canadian Literature/Études en Littérature Canadienne* 15(1): 62-75.

GOTTLIEB, ALLIE. September 26, 2002. "Buffy's Angels", Retrieved 27 July 2007 from *Metroactive.com*.

GRACE. 25 June 2007. "Heroine Content: Feminist and Anti-Racist Thoughts on Women Kicking Ass." *Aliens* (Director's Cut). Retrieved 3 January 2008 from http://www.heroinecontent.net/archives/2007/06/aliens_collectors_edition.html

GRAY, F. Gary (Director). 1996. *Set it Off*. New Line Productions.

HAAG, PAMELA S. 1992. "In Search of 'The Real Thing': Ideologies of Love, Modern Romance, and Women's Sexual Subjectivity in the United States, 1920-40." *Journal of the History of Sexuality*, 2(4): 547-577.

HALBERSTAM, JUDITH. 1998. *Female Masculinity*. Durham and London: Duke University Press.

---. 2005. *In a Queer Time and Place: Transgender Bodies, Subcultural Lives.* New York and London: New York University Press.

HALL, RADCLYFFE. 1928; rpt. 1974. *The Well of Loneliness.* New York: Simon & Schuster, Inc. Pocket Books.

HALL, RADCLYFFE. 1997. *Your John: The Love letters of Radclyffe Hall.*

HAMELIN, CHRISTINE. Nov. 1996. "Self and Other." *Canadian Forum* 75(854): 43-4.

HAMILTON, EDITH AND HUNTINGTON CAIRNS. 1961. *The Collected Dialogues of Plato, Including the Letters.* Pantheon Books: New York.

HARAWAY, DONNA. 1991. "A Cyborg Manifesto: Science, Technology, and Socialist-Feminism in the Late Twentieth Century." In *Simians, Cyborgs and Women: The Reinvention of Nature.* New York; Routledge: 149-181.

HARLIN, RENNY. (Director). 1996. *The Long Kiss Goodnight.* New Line Cinema.

HILLS, ELIZABETH. 1999. "From 'Figurative Males' to Action Heroines: Further Thoughts on Active Women in the Cinema." *Screen,* 40.1: 38-50.

HOGAN, DAVID. (Director). 1996. *Barb Wire.* Universal Studios.

HORNEY, K. 1939. *New Ways in Psychoanalysis.* New York: Norton.

HORRORIST, THE. *Horrorwatch web site.* 2003. Retrieved 12 January 2008 from http://www.horrorwatch.com/ modules/news/article.php?storyid=6

HUTCHINSON, SHARON E. 1996. *Nuer Dilemmas: Coping with Money, War, and the State.* Berkeley: University of California Press.

INNESS, SHERRIE A. (Ed). 2004. *Action Chicks: New Images of*

Tough Women in Popular Culture. New York: Palgrave Macmillan.

INNESS, SHERRIE A. 1999. *Tough Girls: Women Warriors and Wonder Women in Popular Culture.* Philadelphia: University of Philadelphia Press,

JAGOSE, ANNAMARIE. 1996. *Queer Theory: An Introduction.* New York: NYU Press.

JAMES, E. & Mendlesohn, F. (Eds.) 2003. *The Cambridge Companion to Science Fiction.* Cambridge, England: Cambridge University Press.

JEUNET, JEAN-PIERRE. (Director) 1997. *Alien: Resurrection.* Twentieth Century Fox.

JONES, APHRODITE. 1996. *All She Wanted: Brandon Teena: The Girl who Became a Boy but Paid the Ultimate Price.* New York: Simon & Schuster, Inc.

KAUFMAN, MICHAEL. 1987. "The Construction of Masculinity and the Triad of Men's Violence." In Kaufman, Michael, ed. *Beyond Patriarchy: Essays by Men on Pleasure, Power and Changes.* Oxford: Oxford University Press: 1-29.

KOTULA, DEAN. 2002. *The Phallus Palace: Female to Male Transsexuals.* Los Angeles: Alyson Publications.

KRING, TIM. (Director). 2006-2008. *Heroes.* NBC.

KRUPP, CHARLA. June 1992. "She's Bald and She's Back!" *Glamour.* 163.

KUZUI, FRAN RUBEL (DIRECTOR) AND JOSS WHEDON (WRITER). 1992. "Featurette." On Buffy the Vampire Slayer. Twentieth Century Fox.

KUZUI, FRAN RUBEL (DIRECTOR) AND JOSS WHEDON (WRITER). 1992. *Buffy the Vampire Slayer.* Twentieth Century Fox.

LANCASTER, ROGER N. and Micaela di Leonardo. 1997. *The Gender Sexuality Reader: Culture, History, Political Economy.* New York and London: Routledge.

LE GUIN, URSULA K. 1993. *Earthsea Revisioned.* Cambridge, England: Children's Literature New England.

LEE, ANG. (Director). 2000. *Crouching Tiger, Hidden Dragon.* Sony Pictures.

LEVIN, IRA. 1967. *Rosemary's Baby.* NY: Random House.

LUKINBEAL, CHRISTOPHER AND STUART C. Aitken.1998. "Sex, Violence and the Weather: Male Hysteria, Scale and the Fractal Geography of Patriarchy." In Heidi J. Nast, Steve Pile. *Places Through the Body.* Routledge, 1998.

MACDONALD, ANN-MARIE. 1998. *Goodnight Desdemona (Good Morning Juliet).* Toronto: Vintage Canada.

MAGOULICK, MARY. Oct. 2006. "Frustrating Female Heroism: Mixed Messages in *Xena, Nikita,* and *Buffy." Journal of Popular Culture,* 39(5): 729-755.

MARTELL, YAN. 1997. *Self.* Toronto: Random House of Canada Limited.

MCCAUGHEY, MARTHA AND NEAL KING. (Eds.) 2001. *Reel Knockouts: Violent Women in the Movies.* Austin, TX: University of Texas Press.

MCCULLERS, CARSON. 2006. *The Member of the Wedding.* New York, Mariner Books.

MERRICK, H. 2003. "Gender in Science Fiction." In James, E. & Mendlesohn, F. (Eds.) *The Cambridge Companion to Science Fiction:* 241-251. Cambridge: Cambridge University Press.

MILLER, ISABEL. 1973. *Patience and Sarah.* New York: Fawcett Crest.

MITTELMEIER, JENNA. Sept. 2007. "A Generation of Sex Symbols: From *Baywatch* to Britney, Nothing Seems to Shock us Anymore." Retrieved from http://www.kansan.com/stories/2007/sep/21/sex_symbols/

MULVEY, LAURA. Autumn 1975. "Visual Pleasure and

Narrative Cinema." *Screen* 16.3: 6-18.

Munro, Alice. 1968; rpt. 1996. "Boys and Girls." In *Dance of the Happy Shades*. New York: Random House.

Munro, Alice. 1974. *Lives of Girls and Women*. Scarborough, Ontario: Signet.

Muska, Susan and Gréta Olafsdóttir. (Directors). 1998. *The Brandon Teena Story*. Zeitgeist Films.

Nestle, Joan, Clare Howell and Riki Wilchins (Eds.) 2002. *GenderQueer: Voices From Beyond the Sexual Binary*. Los Angeles: Alyson Publications.

Noble, Jean Bobby. 2004. *Masculinities without Men? Female Masculinity in Twentieth Century Fictions*. Vancouver, Canada: UBC Press.

Nova, T. 2007. "G.I. Jane: An Indulgently Butch Army Film." *The Queer Film Review*. Retrieved from http://www.tatenova.com/queerfilm/?p=57

Nussbaum, Martha C. Feb. 22, 1999. "The Professor of Parody: The Hip Defeatism of Judith Butler." *The New Republic*: 37-45.

Pearson, Carol and Katherine Pope. 1981. *The Female Hero in British and American Literature*. New York: Bowker.

Peirce, Kimberly. (Director). 1999. *Boys Don't Cry*. 20th Century Fox.

Pratt, Annis. 1981. *Archetypal Patterns in Women's Fiction*. Bloomington, IN: Indiana University Press

Queen, Carol and Lawrence Schimel (Eds.). 1997. *PoMoSexuals: Challenging Assumptions about Gender and Sexuality*. San Francisco: Cleis Press.

Raimi, Sam (Director). 2002. *Spiderman*. Columbia Pictures.

Ramet, Sabrina Petra, (Ed.) 1996. *Gender Reversals and Gender Cultures: Anthropological and Historical Perspectives*. New York: Routledge.

RIVIERE, JOAN. 1929. "Womanliness as a Masquerade." *International Journal of Psycho-Analysis*, 10: 303-313.

RODENBERRY, GENE. 1966 – 1969. *Star Trek*. NBC.

RODENBERRY, GENE. 1995 – 2001. *Star Trek Voyager*. UPN.

ROSS, SHARON. 2004. "Tough Enough": Female Friendship and Heroism in Xena and Buffy." In Inness, Sherrie A. (Ed). *Action Chicks: New Images of Tough Women in Popular Culture*. New York: Palgrave Macmillan: 231-255.

ROTTNEK, MATTHEW. (Ed.) 1999. *Sissies & Tomboys: Gender Nonconformity & Homosexual Childhood*. New York: New York University Press.

RUSS, JOANNA. 1995. *To Write Like a Woman: Essays in Feminism & Science Fiction*. Bloomington: Indiana University Press.

SALIH, SARA. 2002. *Judith Butler*. London: Routledge.

SCOTT, JOAN WALLACH. 1998. "Gender: A Useful Category of Historical Analysis." *Gender and the Politics of History*. Joan Wallach Scott. (Ed.) New York: Columbia University Press: 28-50.

SCOTT, RIDLEY. (Director). 1979. *Alien*. Twentieth Century Fox.

SCOTT, RIDLEY. (Director). 1997. *GI Jane*. Buena Vista Pictures.

SEDGWICK, EVE KOSOFSKY. 1995. "Gosh, Boy George, You Must be Awfully Secure in your Masculinity!" In Maurice Berger, Brian Wallis, and Simon Watson (Eds.). *Constructing Masculinity*. New York: Routledge: 11-20.

SEXY CARTOON PORN. 2008. Retrieved 17 Nov. 2008 from http://www.sexycartoonporn.net/192/super-hero-porn/wonder-woman-porn.html

SHAKESPEARE, WILLIAM. 1987. *Twelfth Night*. New Revised Edition. New York: Signet Classic Books.

SOMERVILLE, SIOBHAN. 1994. "Scientific Racism and the

Emergence of the Homosexual Body." *Journal of the History of Sexuality* 5(2): 243-266.

SPRETNAK, CHARLENE. 1997. "Radical Nonduality in Ecofeminist Philosophy." In Warren, Karen J. (Ed.) *Ecofeminism: Women, Culture, Nature.* Bloomington and Indianapolis: Indiana University Press: 425-436.

STARTREK.com. 2006. Retrieved 24 Nov. 2007 from http://www.startrek.com/startrek/view/series/TOS/cast/69077.html

SUVIN, DARKO. 1979. *Metamorphoses of Science Fiction .* Yale University Press.

TARANTINO, QUENTIN. (Director). 2004. *Kill Bill*, Vol. 2. Miramax Films.

TARANTINO, QUENTIN. (Director). 2003. *Kill Bill*, Vol. 1. Miramax Films.

TASKER, YVONNE. 2004. *Spectacular Bodies: Gender, Genre and the Action Cinema.* London and New York: Routledge.

THOMPSON, JIM. March 18, 2003. "'Just a girl': Feminism, Postmodernism and Buffy the Vampire Slayer." *Refractory* 2. Retrieved 2 Aug. 2007 from http://blogs.arts.unimelb.edu.au/refractory/2003/03/18/just-a-girl-feminism-postmodernism-and-buffy-the-vampire-slayer-jim-thompson/#more-23

TIME WARNER. Dec. 2, 1999. "The WB Tops Amongst Female Teens in November." Retrieved 8 Dec. 2007 from http://www.timewarner.com/corp/newsroom/pr/0,20812,667569,00.html

TIMMERMAN, J. H. 1983. *Other Worlds: The Fantasy Genre.* Bowling Green, OH: Bowling Green State University Popular Press.

TREMAIN, ROSE. 1992. *Sacred Country.* London: Sinclair-Stevenson.

TUNG, CHARLENE. 2004. "Embodying an Image: Gender, Race and Sexuality in La Femme Nikita." *Action Chicks: New Images of Tough Women in Popular Culture.* Sherrie A. Inness. (Ed.) New York: Palgrave Macmillan: 95-121.

TWO SIDES TO NOWHERE. 30 May, 2007. "Frustrating Female Feminism: Missing the Point." Retrieved 15 July 2008 from http://twosidestonowhere.blogspot. com/2007/05/frustrating-female-feminism-missing. html

USSHER, JANE M. 1997. *Fantasies of Femininity: Reframing the Boundaries of Sex.* Rutgers University Press.

VENTURA, HELIANE. 1992. "Alice Munro's 'Boys and Girls': Mapping Out Boundaries." *Commonwealth Essays and Studies* 15(1): 80-87.

WEST, SIMON. (Director). 2001. *Tomb Raider.* Paramount Pictures.

WHEDON, JOSS. (Creator/Director/Writer). 1997 – 2003. *Buffy the Vampire Slayer* Television Series. Warner Bros (1st five seasons); United Paramount Network (last 2 seasons).

WHEDON, JOSS. (Creator/Director/Writer). 2002 – 2003. *Firefly* Television Series. Fox Broadcasting Company.

WHEDON, JOSS. 1997. "Interview with Joss Whedon & David Boreanaz." On Joss Whedon, *Buffy the Vampire Slayer* Television Series on DVD, Season 1, Disk 1.

WILCHINS, RIKI. 2002. "A Continuous Nonverbal Communication." In *GenderQueer: Voices From Beyond the Sexual Binary.* Joan Nestle, Clare Howell and Riki Wilchins (Eds). Los Angeles: Alyson Publications: 11–17.

WILCOX, FRED M. (Director). 1956. *Forbidden Planet.* Metro-Goldwyn-Mayer.

www.ingramcontent.com/pod-product-compliance
Lightning Source LLC
Chambersburg PA
CBHW072247270326
41930CB00010B/2291